"*Light in the Darkness: Preparing Better Catholic Funerals* is a succinct and thoughtful presentation of the Church's liturgical theology of her funeral rites. Clergy, pastoral associates, musicians, and all who are entrusted with the planning of Catholic funerals will find this work to be an engaging and helpful pastoral resource. Fr. Turner's vast experience as a liturgical scholar and pastor shine forth in this valuable guide."

> — Fr. Matthew Ernest
> Director of the Office of Liturgy, Archdiocese of New York
> Professor and Director of Liturgy, St. Joseph's Seminary,
> Dunwoodie

"*Light in the Darkness* is an utterly practical manual based on the author's long experience as a pastor. This shows in the way it begins with a section on Pastoral Care before moving on to look at rituals and provide practical resources. What a treasure box the 'Toolbox' section is, particularly for clergy."

> — Elizabeth Harrington
> Education Officer
> Liturgy Brisbane

Light in the Darkness

Preparing Better Catholic Funerals

Paul Turner

LITURGICAL PRESS
Collegeville, Minnesota

www.litpress.org

1	2	3	4	5	6	7	8	9

Library of Congress Cataloging-in-Publication Data

Names: Turner, Paul, 1953– author.
Title: Light in the darkness : preparing better Catholic funerals / Paul Turner.
Description: Collegeville, Minnesota : Liturgical Press, 2017.
Identifiers: LCCN 2017004822 (print) | LCCN 2017026360 (ebook) |
    ISBN 9780814646311 (ebook) | ISBN 9780814646076 (paperback)
Subjects: LCSH: Funeral service—Catholic Church. | Catholic Church. Order
    of Christian funerals. | Death—Religious aspects—Catholic Church.
Classification: LCC BX2035.6.F853 (ebook) | LCC BX2035.6.F853 T87 2017
    (print) | DDC 264/.020985—dc23
LC record available at https://lccn.loc.gov/2017004822

AVCTOR DEDICAT HVNC VOLVMEN
AD MEMORIAM SVBRINI SVI
STEPHANI BERTRAND
CVM QVO IN PVERITIA
REPSIT AMBVLAVIT LVSIT ET VOCATIONES CREVIT
CVIVS SEMITA AD SEDEM DIVERSAM DVXIT
CVIVS CEREBRVM SIGNATVM EST
MAGIS PRO INGENIO QVAM INFIRMITATE
QVI NON TIMVIT QVANDO ADVENIT MORS
ET CVM QVO IPSE SPERAT
VT CONVENIAT ET AD VITAM ÆTERNAM
RESVRGAT

Contents

Acknowledgments

I wish to thank

the Dioceses of Lubbock, Perth, Shreveport, Biloxi, and Greensburg, who invited,

Steve Pierce and Charlie Passantino, who shared,

Mike and Carol Mathews, who waited,

Cathy Hernández and Peg Ekerdt, who read,

and God, who promises eternal life.

Preface

Funerals are a service that Catholic parishes offer to human society. They enshrine a person's life in ceremonies that bring honor to the deceased and bestow hope on the mourners. They gather family and friends to sacred space where together they contemplate the very mystery of life and death.

Although the Catholic funeral rites have not changed much since the early 1970s, society has. In the past, both liturgically and culturally, funerals followed a predictable pattern. The wake, the funeral Mass, and the cemetery service formed a familiar threefold structure. The chants were predetermined and remarkably well known: *Requiem æternam, Dies iræ, Lux æterna,* and *In paradisum,* for example. Members of many parishes provided mourners with funeral dinners of traditional local fare.

After the Second Vatican Council the Catholic Church broadened a funeral's selection of readings, prayers, music, ministries, and services. A grieving family faces still more options at the funeral home. The winds of social change have made an impact as well, where secular influences arise in such areas as an expedient schedule of services, a simpler disposition of the remains, nonecclesial places of gathering, a shift in purpose from Christian hope to humanist celebration, and a preference for those who are not clergy to speak in memory of the deceased.

The post–Vatican II Catholic funeral rite in English, released in 1971, revised in 1981, and given an appendix in 1997, has undergone relatively little alteration. Although other liturgical books have entered second and third editions and received revised vernacular translations, *The Order of Christian Funerals* (OCF) has remained basically the same.

Funerals have not. The Catholic Church has lost its grip over the traditional three stages of ceremonies, the management of music, and the content and presenter of eulogies. A parish does not have much control over many decisions that mourners make. In the midst of these changes, this book offers suggestions for improving parish ministry toward those who may have lost connections with Catholic traditions and piety. Its primary purposes are (1) to prepare the faithful in advance for decisions that they will face when a loved one dies and (2) to help them celebrate funerals well. Those strategies may help mourners think not only of their memories of the deceased person but also of the church to which he or she belonged. A funeral will help family, friends, church, and community move through the grief of loss, from darkness into light.

I'm the pastor of a Catholic parish in the middle of the United States. If you are a priest, deacon, parish staff member, musician, or volunteer who helps with funerals, may God bless you for your service. I hope to help you guide your flock in preparing better Catholic funerals.

Pastoral Care

1

The Person Who Died

Normally the person for whom a parish prepares a funeral is a Catholic (canon 1176 §1). Ideally, this person was an active member of the local church, perhaps raised a family there, worshiped there regularly, made friends, and served in ministerial capacities. A funeral at church is the logical conclusion to the life of such a person. All the values and faith that guided one's life move inexorably toward a final farewell inside the building that served as one's center of moral gravity. Parish ministers cherish such a funeral because it also confirms the values that they hold. Ministers are committed to parish life, they encourage others to share their enthusiasm, and they feel affirmed when members get involved. When a faithful Catholic dies, the funeral rites cohere effortlessly.

It does not always work that way, however. Some baptized Catholics have a more tangential relationship to the parish church. They may not even know the name of the pastor. Other reasons may have brought them there for the funeral: a connection to the parish in the past, ethnic or racial traditions associated with the parish, or the previous funerals of other family members. Parish ministers often find these funerals more difficult. They may not know the family and may feel disconnected from the person's life. Funerals are always an inconvenience in a well-planned week, but these funerals feel even more so. Ministers may actually feel resentful that a person who did not contribute much to the life and ministry of the parish now requires attention from those who do. Still, every deceased Catholic has a right to a funeral Mass, and parish ministers promote the gospel of mercy when they graciously assist those who mourn Catholics who were living at the church's margins.

Sometimes the parish has no record of the person who died. Ministers expect people to register with their parish. Registration creates a record of those who belong to that local church. It promotes commitment, community, giving, service, and celebration. Registration helps the staff understand whom they have in the pews and in the homes. But not everyone registers. In the Hispanic Catholic community, for example, the parish church is home. People don't register to enter their own home, so they may not think of registering at church. Even so, at times like a funeral, ministers will often check to see if the person who died was a registered member. Some families have no idea that they are not registered. They may assume that they can obtain the services of the church of their choice as surely as they can obtain services from any funeral home. If they are already overwhelmed with grief, a parish minister's question about registration may sound callous, making preparations even more difficult.

Parishes have boundaries that distribute the Catholic population into accessible districts. No matter where a family lives or how inactive its members are, they have a parish and a pastor because of boundaries. Today, however, those boundaries have become porous. Catholics "shop" for the church that best suits their needs, and they travel there even if it requires a longer commute. For those with special needs ranging from physical accessibility to native languages, the commute may even be longer because the choice of parish is more limited.

As a pastor, I am a strong believer in parish registration, and I remind people to update their status. Still, I have always felt a duty toward those who live within the parish boundaries. Even if they never registered with us, the boundaries grant assurance that they have a local pastor responsible for them, simply because of where they live. These funerals can be especially inopportune, but I feel that they are part of my responsibilities.

Catechumens also have a right to a Catholic funeral (canon 1183 §1). No one hopes to face this circumstance. Catechumens are looking forward to their baptism, not to their death. If a catechumen is dying, a priest need not wait for Easter to baptize. The Rite of Christian Initiation of Adults (RCIA) includes a chapter called "Christian Initiation of a Person in Danger of Death" especially for this circumstance (part II, sect. 3, para. 370–99). However, some people die unexpectedly, even tragically. If death comes to a catechumen, parishes offer the pastoral care and liturgical services appropriate for a member of the Catholic family.

Parishes can protect this right by having two plans in place: the regular celebration of the Rite of Acceptance into the Order of Catechumens and a register of catechumens maintained in the parish office. The Rite of Acceptance unequivocally establishes a person as a catechumen. Making this opportunity available at different times of the year can ensure that those inquiring about Christianity can be numbered among its flock in the broadest sense. After the ceremony, their names should be entered into a roll of catechumens in the parish office in a book that resembles a baptismal register. Some individuals who begin the spiritual formation of the catechumenate discontinue it because of disinterest or conflicting responsibilities and values. However, they are still catechumens. Often they have not yet registered as members of the parish, but they have a status within the community, and some record should be made.

A child who dies before an intended baptism causes unimaginable grief in the lives of parents, family, and friends. Parents deserve the consolation and support of the parish. Some parents in this circumstance instinctively want to avoid a formal funeral. The grief is already too much to bear. Especially in the case of a child who died *in utero*, the remains may be irretrievably lost. But for those who desire a ceremony, the parish may offer a funeral for a child who dies before baptism where the local ordinary has permitted it (canon 1183 §2).

In the past, Catholics learned that the souls of such children went to limbo, a place short of heaven, because they were never baptized. Many Catholics found this teaching an invitation to despair. In 2007 the Vatican's International Theological Commission investigated the question and published a statement, "The Hope of Salvation for Infants Who Die without Being Baptized." The title summarizes the conclusion: the commission taught that Catholics have a well-founded hope—not assurance—in the salvation of these infants. The Vatican apparently tried to lift people out of the realms of despair, but it could not do so completely because of the theological difficulty that the gateway to salvation is baptism. The *Catechism of the Catholic Church* issues the same message of hope of salvation (1261), not of its confident assurance. Some Catholics may say that they are untroubled by such teachings past and present. Their faith assures them that an innocent child who dies without baptism still passes from death to eternal life. When it happens to them, however, when a child in their family—or of their own—dies before an intended baptism, doubts may arise. In such cases a funeral Mass with a burial service may offer consolation in a ritual that goes beyond mere words.

On occasion, when a non-Catholic dies, the family may ask about having the funeral in a Catholic parish. For example, a person baptized in another Christian denomination may have a Catholic spouse and have assisted in many events at the Catholic parish. If such non-Catholics have not retained connections to the church of their baptism, they or their families may ask if the Catholic parish can assist at the time of death. The parish may offer a funeral in this case if the local ordinary judges it prudent, as long as the deceased did not have a contrary intention and if the proper minister is unavailable (canon 1183 §3; OCF 18). At times this outreach seems most compassionate and even logical if the deceased has been known in the local Catholic community.

There is no canonical provision for offering a Catholic funeral to a non-Christian. However, the American edition of the OCF includes a prayer for this circumstance if the person was married to a Catholic (398 §36). Perhaps this presumes that the person was a catechumen.

The Catholic Church denies funerals to individuals who belong to certain groups: notorious apostates, heretics, and schismatics; those who choose cremation for reasons opposed to Christianity, such as disbelief in the resurrection of the body; and manifest sinners who may cause scandal to the faithful—unless the person in question showed some signs of repentance before death (canon 1184 §1). In general, though, pastors should not be too quick to deny Christian burial. Church services may offer consolation to the family, and, as will be seen, Catholic funerals do not presume the moral uprightness of any of the deceased. Everyone sins.

The basic structure and content of Catholic funerals is the same for everyone, sinner and saint, wastrel and pope. The commonality of the prayers equalizes every deceased Christian, as does the pall that covers the coffin. We all end life as we began it—humans like all others.

By the way, I've decided to use the word "coffin" instead of "casket" throughout this book simply because that is the word used in the OCF.

Funeral Homes and Cemeteries

Employees at a funeral home and at cemeteries provide an invaluable service to families and parishes alike. A good working relationship between the parish staff and the funeral home ensures the smooth celebration of the funeral rites and seamless ministry to those who grieve.

Most of those who manage funeral homes and parishes want this kind of relationship. Everyone truly cares about serving families in the best way. Funeral directors have their own challenges—especially from people making unusual, emotional requests. It helps to establish some procedures with the funeral homes that ensure the most contact with the parish church. This especially pertains when a new pastor comes to the parish. Even though the OCF is identical in every parish, each priest celebrates funerals a little differently.

A funeral home often receives news about a deceased Catholic before the parish does, and at times plans for services have advanced before the parish has a chance to consult the family. Depending on the funeral home, an employee may have reviewed a number of liturgical considerations with the family even before contacting the priest. This is most effective when funeral home employees have learned the preferences of individual priests and parishes and put them in practice.

Someone at the funeral home has worked with the family on the expenses incurred. Sometimes the person who has died paid for all expenses in advance, even decades earlier. Other times there is no plan at all. Almost every family expects expenses at the funeral home, but some families are surprised to learn that the parish also expects a financial offering. A parish can help everyone by drafting a policy that families may review. For example, a parish may hope for stipends to be paid to the priest, deacon, musicians, servers, the organization preparing a lunch, or the parish in general. A policy could state sample stipends or a range of gifts that have been given in the past. Some musicians prefer a set fee for their services; if so, it is fair to list their names and the amount requested. If it seems appropriate, such a policy could conclude with a statement such as this: "These figures are suggestions intended to assist the grieving family's plans. They are adjusted down for those suffering financial burdens. Other families prefer to offer more. Every gift is gratefully received."

Parishes have an obligation to bury the dead, regardless of payment, yet many people want to make an appropriate gift to the parish at this pivotal moment in family history. A policy posted on the website and placed in the hands of funeral directors will ease the way.

> If you have not done so, it is a good idea to meet with a funeral director about the plans for your own funeral. Apart from having personal benefits for you and your family, this brings professional benefits. You will understand better what the people in the parish are experiencing when they make plans for the funerals of those they love, and for themselves.

Cemetery staffs operate independently of funeral homes, but in concert with them. The funeral home often, though not always, facilitates the interrelationship of cemetery and parish staffs. As will be seen, the Catholic funeral provides some options at the cemetery, such as having people witness the interment of the remains. Ministers should know exactly what needs to happen in case of such requests.

Some cemeteries are owned and managed by dioceses and parishes. Cemetery boards typically take their work seriously and want to provide for the perpetual care of the remains of the people their community loved. Once again, a good working relationship with such boards will facilitate pastoral care and forestall problems.

The Obituary

People rarely consult the parish at the time of writing the obituary. Usually the funeral home offers assistance. Parish ministers may offer general advice in conversations with funeral directors and parishioners. For example, the liturgical names of the usual services are the "Vigil for the Deceased," the "Funeral Mass," and the "Rite of Committal" (OCF 54, 154, and 216). Sometimes people use other expressions in obituaries, such as "wake service," "Celebration of Life," "Mass of Christian Burial," "Mass of the Resurrection," or "Memorial Mass." These are imprecise designations, as will be discussed below. Dioceses or parishes may develop policies for the terminology they prefer in the obituaries of Catholics, though in reality people who read them will probably understand the commonly used terms.

Beyond terminology, other aspects of Catholic life may earn a mention in an obituary. If the deceased person was active in the parish church, some record of this participation would serve both as a tribute to the person's service and as an inspiration to those who survive. Many families recommend charities where their friends may make donations in memory of the deceased. Among these they may list the name of the parish church. If they do so, parish ministers owe the family personal thanks.

From time to time ministers may inform parishioners about the options for giving at the end of life. People can have their money or property donated to a charity at the moment of their death. They may remember the parish in their will. Even if the parish receives only a small amount, it diversifies the ways that people can give, promotes better stewardship, and gives people the satisfaction of knowing that in dying they are still giving for the sake of the gospel. It can also add a small though significant stream of income for the parish.

However, obituaries are expensive. A local newspaper may allow a few dozen words without cost, but then charge for additional words and a photo. Some families therefore authorize the newspaper to publish a short obituary that directs the reader to the website of the funeral home for more information. Many funeral homes offer free space on their sites for longer obituaries. In extreme cases, a long obituary published on multiple days in a major newspaper, or in several papers, can cost more than the services of a funeral home.

If the parish has a way of sending news out to parishioners either through social media or an email distribution list, the family of the deceased may appreciate it if the parish shares news of the death, the request for prayers, and an electronic link to the obituary. The obituary could also appear in a program printed for the funeral.

Planning the Ceremonies

Preparations for funeral liturgies best include face-to-face conversation between someone at the parish and one or more of the mourners. Even when ministers know the deceased person very well, they can learn more from family members who see the person's life more totally and can begin to interpret its meaning. This meeting concerns pastoral care as well as funeral details. This blend of compassion and organization helps many mourners feel that someone cares for them and is guiding them through important decisions pertaining to someone they loved. Depending on the circumstances, here are some topics to discuss:

- The events at the time of death. This is often uppermost in the minds of the mourners. The parish minister may invite them to tell the story of how the person died. "Who was present? Were you there? What do you remember? If you weren't there, how did you learn about the death? What was that like?" The moment of death is a sacred moment, so letting people tell the story will help the minister step into their lives.

- The career. "How did the deceased person dedicate his or her life? Was there one job or several? How did this person make an impact on society? How important was school? Military service? Community service?"

- Family role. Beyond the career, discuss the person's role in the family. "How was she as a mother?" "What kind of dad was he?" Or if the spouse survives, "How many years were you together? How was he (she) as a companion for life? What are your favorite memories of this person's role in your family?"

- Biographical details. The minister may ask about the person's youth, school activities, hobbies, pastimes—anything that will give an insight into the person and how the family will remember his or her life. Some family members tell stories of success; others remember stories of struggle.

I take notes on all of this to help me minister to this family and to prepare the homily. When I preach, I don't give a complete report of everything I've learned, but I often share some of the fruits of this conversation. I believe it adds depth and consolation to the homily.

Some mourners may agree to take part in the ceremonies. Here are some roles that they may fill:

- Placing the pall. When the coffin arrives at the church, a large white pall is placed on top. Members of the family may perform this gesture.

- Selecting the readings. Some family members want to spend time thinking about the passages to be proclaimed at the vigil for the deceased or at the funeral Mass. If so, they may be given a list of citations to review, or someone from the parish may suggest a smaller list of readings that seem especially pertinent. The chart in the Toolbox section of this book will help (see pp. 97–99). Such conversations help family members dialogue between the life of the person they've lost and the living word of God. When they hear one of these readings at some other event in the future, they may recall more clearly that they chose it for this funeral. Other times, family members prefer that the priest or someone from the parish choose the citations on their behalf. They may have so many decisions to make already that having someone else choose the readings offers relief.

- Proclaiming the readings. Scriptures may be proclaimed at the vigil for the deceased, the funeral Mass, and at the cemetery. If someone already serving as a reader at Sunday Mass is a member of the family or close friend, that person makes the best choice. Sometimes others with little or no experience of reading in public offer to perform this function. Sometimes it works. Sometimes it does not. People may not know when to approach the ambo for a reading, how to execute the reverences customary to the local community, where to find the reading, and how to use a microphone. Funerals are emotional; some people may not realize how difficult it could be for them to stand up in public in front of a microphone and read—without dissolving into tears. A skilled reader will usually be up to the challenge.

- Procession of the gifts. Ideally, the people presenting the bread and wine at a funeral Mass are among those who will be receiving communion. The offerings, which will be consecrated and returned to the people in communion, are a sign of the sacrifice of the community. Sometimes people like to involve non-Catholic members of the family or friends because they are ineligible for communion. Inviting them to bring up the gifts but not receive communion, however, is a bit like inviting people to bring food over for dinner but not to stay and eat it.

- Communion ministers. If there are extraordinary ministers of holy communion among the family and friends, they may help with communion at a funeral Mass. If not, these ministers may be drawn from the parish community.

- Musicians. Normally it is best to let the parish musicians lead the singing. They are most familiar with repertoire and with liturgical guidelines. Still, if a family member or friend wishes to contribute music to the event, this can be discussed. The primary singers at a funeral, however, are the members of the assembly, not a soloist.

- Ushers and greeters. As people arrive for the funeral, first-time visitors to the church will appreciate having someone at the doors to welcome them and answer any questions about the building and the upcoming service. This may be as simple as directing people to restrooms or as complex as explaining the building's art and architecture.

- Servers. The parish altar servers usually make the best choice for this ministry at a funeral Mass. However, on occasion there may be altar servers in the family who could help. If the funeral takes place during school hours, it may difficult to find children available for this ministry. Adult servers often fulfill this role capably.

You may want to prepare a simple form listing the possible ways for people to become involved. Print it on parish stationery with an email address where the family can return the names of the people they suggest. Let them take the form home and think it over.

You may also schedule time for the readers to practice in church with a competent reader from the parish.

What We Are Doing

The main liturgical celebration after a Catholic dies is the funeral Mass. That is its title in the OCF. Not all use it. For example, some people refer to this Mass as a "Celebration of Life." The title can be seen in obituaries and funeral programs, and it can be heard in announcements and greetings. The title "Celebration of Life" appears to serve two purposes: it aims to change the mood from grief to celebration, and it looks back with favor over the life lived, rather than forward in hope over the life to come.

Other Catholics and parishes call the ceremony the "Mass of the Resurrection." This seems to render a final favorable judgment on the eternal salvation of the deceased. There are problems with this designation, of course. First of all, God—not the parish—is the judge of human life. The question of resurrection is in God's hands, and the prayers of the funeral liturgy acknowledge this with respect and humility. The obituary and the parish funeral program should not usurp the role of Christ the judge of the world. Another difficulty is that "Mass of the Resurrection" resembles the title that the Missal uses for another occasion: Easter Sunday of the Resurrection of the Lord, Mass during the Day. If there is a Mass of the Resurrection, it's Easter. And it's the Mass of the *Lord's* resurrection.

Another common designation is the term "Memorial Mass," which usually indicates a Mass after burial at which the mourners are present, but not the body. The OCF never uses this term. The Missal simply calls it a "Mass for the Dead." One could argue that it is the funeral Mass because there is no other one, even though this Mass does not include the extra rites that pertain to the body. The term "Memorial Mass," however, is broadly used and understood, even though the official liturgy does not employ the title.

The term "Mass of Christian Burial" probably evolved to distinguish it from the "Memorial Mass." It indicates the Mass with the remains of the deceased present in the church. Of course, not every deceased Catholic is being buried, as will be discussed below. Some remains are placed in mausoleums or columbaria, and some ashes are kept privately or scattered in the open. The OCF does not use the expression "Mass of Christian Burial," which now seems prescient, given the later developments in the disposition of remains. It consistently uses the term "Funeral Mass."

The preconciliar funeral rite conveyed a sense of contrition and fear. The priest wore black vestments, which seemed to underscore the sadness of death. The music included the *Dies iræ*, the sequence that was sung before the gospel introducing themes of fear about the final judgment and the potential day of wrath that awaited a deceased, unrepentant sinner. After Vatican II, the funeral liturgy turned its course in another direction, framing the pertinent rites within one of the council's favorite themes: the paschal mystery. Whereas past Catholic piety may have dwelled too intently on the cross, the paschal mystery embraces both cross and resurrection, reality and hope.

Some people, however, have turned the funeral rites into mini-canonization proceedings, celebrating resurrection before any divine judgment could possibly be known. The paschal mystery is not just the mystery of the resurrection any more than it is just the mystery of the cross. It is both. And within that dynamic lies true Catholic faith.

What we are doing at a funeral, then, is praying for the soul of the one who has died. Instead of proclaiming with assurance that the deceased is now in heaven, the Catholic funeral liturgy proclaims hope in the resurrection, places judgment in God's hands, and prays fervently on behalf of the deceased. I try to make the words of comfort I speak privately consonant with the words of hope I speak publicly at the funeral Mass. You'll find more on this in the remarks on the homily below.

Cremation

The Catholic Church permits cremation, as long as it is not chosen for anti-Catholic purposes (canon 1176 §3), such as disbelief in the resurrection of the body or a belief that one's material body is not sacred. People sometimes view the Catholic Church's hesitations about cremation as antiquated. The American Catholic bishops realized that the OCF did not sufficiently treat cremation, so their Committee on the Liturgy published an appendix that included "Reflections on the Body, Cremation, and Catholic Funeral Rites."

These first laid out arguments in favor of burial, which is the ancient Christian custom (OCF 19). After all, this is the body that received the sacraments and awaits the final resurrection, as the church proclaims each Sunday in the Creed. These points are made in the appendix to the Order of Christian Funerals (OCFa 412). Saint Paul wrote that Christ would change our lowly body to conform with his glorified body (Phil 3:21), and that, just as our body bore the image of the earthly Jesus, so it will also bear his image in heaven (1 Cor 15:49). Even though nearly half of Americans were choosing cremation in the first decades of the twenty-first century, the Catholic Church prefers that the body be present for the funeral rites (OCFa 413).

Nonetheless, the bishops permitted cremation when "extraordinary circumstances" make it "the only feasible choice" (OCFa

415). It is no secret that people are choosing cremation not when it is the only feasible choice, but in quite ordinary circumstances when other choices exist. They choose cremation for its simplicity, its lower cost, the flexibility to choose the date for the funeral, environmental concerns, space available in a preferred cemetery, and the options it provides for the final disposition of one's remains. These reasons are serious, well considered, and based on values that of themselves cohere with Catholic morality.

But the American bishops' dossier of reasons for displaying a complete dead body at a vigil service, receiving a body in church, and burying a body in a cemetery is impressive:

- Seeing the body confronts people with the mystery of life and death.

- The body naturally recalls stories of faith, family and friendship, the words a person spoke, the deeds a person performed.

- Although we have virtual electronic friendships, people best encounter another person through the body.

- The body experienced the sacraments: being washed in baptism and anointed in confirmation, and by eating and drinking the body and blood of Christ in communion.

- The body is destined for the glory of the resurrection.

- The final care of the body demonstrates dignity for the whole person.

- Burial imitates the burial of Jesus' body, and thus constitutes another layer of discipleship (see OCFa 411–12).

Before opting for cremation, Christians do well to consider the significance of the body, its impact upon mourners, the memories it summons, and the hope it promises to faithful disciples of Christ.

Some crematoriums permit mourners to be present at the time of cremation. Not many people ask for this, but if they do, it may be possible for them to sit next to the furnace, or in an adjacent room. There they may be at prayer and in reflection, present to the one they love, while the ashes are prepared.

The OCF never uses the popular term "cremains," preferring instead the more descriptive expression "cremated remains." At first sounding like a mere circumlocution, this expression puts the emphasis on the word "remains." The community is dealing with the remains of a human body. The word "cremains" removes the reality one step further. The liturgical vocabulary strives mightily to help people remember that this is a human person.

The church permits cremation perhaps in surrender to societal norms and preferences, even among faithful Catholics. Regarding the sequence of Catholic liturgical events involving a cremation, there are three possibilities:

1. *Cremation takes place after the funeral (OCFa 418–21).* The church prefers this option because it allows the body to be present for the vigil for the deceased and the funeral Mass. The symbols and prayers of Catholic funerals, passed down through centuries of observance, all predate the accessibility and popularity of cremation, and they presume that mourners have gathered in the presence of the body. In this case the body may be set inside a removable interior, placed inside a ceremonial coffin—one that the funeral home may use again on another occasion. The body is presented inside this coffin for the viewing by family and friends, creating a better final memory for them. The final commendation and farewell take place at the funeral Mass as usual, but the trip to the cemetery is delayed. The body is taken to the crematorium instead. Employees lift the coffin's removable interior along with the body, place these in the crematorium, and begin the process. Afterward, they gather the ashes into an urn. The final step, the interment of the ashes, takes place at a later time. The church prefers this sequence of events because of the respect it holds for the body. Some Catholics do choose this.

2. *Cremation and committal take place before the funeral Mass (OCFa 422–25).* In this option, not only is the body not present for the funeral Mass; the ashes are not there either. The OCFa lists

this as the second option, which implies that it is the church's second preference. Perhaps this recalls the older tradition that Catholics were not cremated, so it would seem inopportune to have the cremated remains present for a funeral Mass. In fact, that was still the case prior to 1997, when the American bishops first began to permit funeral Masses with the ashes present in the church. The second option shares the view of the former practice: the ashes are not in church for the Mass. They have already been interred. The Mass is what is commonly called a memorial Mass, which the Missal calls a "Mass for the Dead." However, the selection of prayers needs to avoid those that make explicit references to a body in statements such as "whose body we honor with Christian burial" (OCF 164c).

3. *The funeral Mass takes place with the ashes present (OCFa 426–31).* The third option, seemingly the least preferred by the OCF, is the one that Catholics very frequently select. In this case, the cremated remains are to be placed inside a worthy vessel. Sometimes the family receives them from the crematorium in a cardboard box. Some churches or funeral homes have a reusable urn for such occasions. Visually, the vessel for the remains should look dignified and worthy of respect. It contains what remains of a human person. The vessel may be carried to the church solemnly in procession and placed on a small table in the area that the coffin normally occupies. If this option is chosen, the paschal candle stands by the remains, as it does at a funeral with the body present (OCFa 435).

One of the most serious difficulties in Catholic funerals is the final placement of the cremated remains of the deceased. Trending practices in the culture promote two extremes: the very personal and the very public.

In the first instance, some people keep the remains of their loved ones in an urn at home on a mantle. If a person has lost a spouse, a child, or a parent, for example, this provides one way that a mourner can keep the loved one present at all times. Even more personal is locking ashes inside jewelry. Because of a similar aversion to loss, mourners can wear the remains of their loved ones. This has also prompted the practice of dividing the remains among various mourners, so that each can have part of the one who has died.

On the opposite end are those who prefer a very public disposition of the ashes. They may be poured into the sea, launched from the air, scattered upon the ground, or released in the wind. These practices disperse the ashes to the widest possible margins, in direct contrast to the practice of keeping them close at home. Some people like the thought that their remains will forever rest scattered in a place beloved to them.

These decisions are usually made with considerable forethought, and they represent a certain belief about the sacredness of the remains, their significance to the closest members of the family, or their relationship to the mystery of the great outdoors. Probably not many are thinking about their belief in the resurrection of the body that they profess each Sunday at Mass. Of these two extremes, the retention of ashes underscores the intimacy of human love, whereas the scattering of ashes professes the uncontainable mystery of human life.

The Vatican approves neither practice. In 2016 the Congregation for the Doctrine of the Faith (CDF) issued its instruction *Ad resurgendum cum Christo*: Regarding the Burial of the Deceased and the Conservation of the Ashes in the Case of Cremation. It reviewed the principal Catholic teachings about death and resurrection, noted current practices, and then restated and expanded the pertinent restrictions. It acknowledges that cremation may be chosen for "sanitary, economic or social considerations" (4), but these should not violate the wishes of the deceased person.

The CDF requires that ashes be laid to rest in a sacred place, such as a cemetery or a church in order to ensure remembrance by the family and community and to prevent a lack of respect, which could become more likely in subsequent generations entrusted with ashes at home. Committal to a public place also prevents superstitious practices (5).

Consequently, "the conservation of the ashes of the departed in a domestic residence is not permitted," nor is the division of ashes among family members (6). Ashes should not be scattered, in order to avoid any appearance of pantheism, naturalism, or nihilism, nor may they be preserved in jewelry or other objects (7). "When the deceased notoriously has requested cremation and the scattering of their ashes for reasons contrary to the Christian faith, a Christian funeral must be denied to that person according to the norms of the law" (8). This final statement runs the danger of misinterpretation. It does not prevent the Christian funeral of anyone desiring the scattering of ashes, but only of those who do it for reasons contrary to the Christian faith.

Still, a great many of the Catholic faithful will neither learn about this teaching nor observe it. They may be familiar with friends of other Christian congregations whose authorities find no conflict between these practices and faith in Christ. Catholic pastors can preach reminders, but they are nearly helpless in enforcing a prohibition of the conservation, preservation, or distribution of ashes. Employees at Catholic funeral homes can repeat the message when they visit with the family of those who have died. But the power over the remains is in the hands of others. A pastor can and should educate the faithful, but he cannot always change their plans, especially when death has come and the decisions have long been made.

Some people consider the CDF's statement on cremation hypocrisy when considering the Catholic Church's practice of honoring the relics of saints. After all, parts of the saints have been divided and shared among the faithful, many of them encased in jewelry. Indeed, there are parallels. The desire of the Christian faithful to be in the presence of some part of a saint is not unlike the desire of family members to be in the presence of some part of a deceased member.

The main difference is that the relics of saints are meant for public veneration. It is true that many of them are in private hands, but Rome discourages the private ownership of relics. The distribution of relics falls to the liturgical office of the vicariate of Rome.

Its Norms for the Concession of Relics kept in the Reliquary of the Diocese of Rome (Prot. N. 10/09) permit the distribution of relics only for the sake of public veneration.

This differs from the practice of putting ashes on a mantle at home or in a piece of jewelry to be worn by an individual. People may do something similar with relics, but the practice is discouraged. Relics are retained for public devotion, not private usage.

The Absence of the Body

Some people donate their body to science. At some point, science may return what remains of the body to the family. If possible, the funeral rite would fittingly take place before the body is sent away, in order that the community may pay its respects. However, if that is not possible, the community may gather for a ceremony without the presence of the body. This is a simple Mass for the dead from the Missal, or as many people call it, a memorial Mass. Then, if and when the remains are returned, final interment may take place with the rite of committal at the cemetery.

In some tragic circumstances, nothing remains of the body at all. Sometimes the fate is known because of witnesses to an explosion, for example. At other times, the fate is unknown, as in the case of prisoners of war, soldiers missing in action, or people in nonmilitary situations who have alarmingly disappeared without explanation. When, sadly, there is no trace of the deceased and death is presumed, a funeral Mass can and should still be held. Obviously, the family will require sensitive pastoral care.

The Three Stages

The Catholic Church recommends services in three stages: the vigil for the deceased, the funeral Mass, and the rite of committal. Many families, however, are requesting only two or even just one of these. Frequently the vigil is eliminated, and the family hosts a visitation in church just before the funeral Mass. At a visitation, mourners may informally greet and console members of the family. At other times, all the services are held at the funeral home or at the cemetery. The traditional three stages are breaking down in American Catholic society.

Social media have introduced additional means of expressing grief. When a friend on Facebook dies, for example, people write words of condolence—some about the deceased, and some *to* the deceased. If the name has not been removed from Facebook, birthday announcements will go out as usual. Friends then fall into two categories: those who remembered the death and those who did not know. The first group sends messages of grief; the others send greetings of joy. Funeral homes also provide websites where people may send messages of compassion to the bereaved. Such services allow mourners to form a virtual community, especially those who are unable to attend the funeral.

It may be helpful to review for people the purpose of the three stages. The processions mirror the journey of the Christian life (OCF 42). They join the different elements of the liturgy and help the faithful to enter its meaning. The OCF recommends that the pallbearers actually carry the coffin (41). This will not always be practical, but it would help drive home the physical action of making a pilgrimage.

Three stages also give other mourners options for when they can see the family. Many people are available only in the evenings, and they prefer that opportunity for gathering in prayer and for the social conventions of shared grief. Others wish to participate in the funeral Mass during the day. A smaller but significant group will process all the way to the cemetery. The three stages thus provide pastoral care for those who grieve.

Grieving families often do not see it that way. Some of them prefer a more expedient use of their time. They miss the one they loved, of course, but death has inconvenienced their usual routine. By condensing the visitation with the funeral, or eliminating the funeral Mass altogether in favor of a service at the funeral home or cemetery, grieving families concede to the busyness of their lives and the desire to move beyond disquieting thoughts of death.

In a culture where some of the closest friendships are sustained electronically, where members of a younger generation therefore do not value being physically present with an older family member, where some individuals work more than one job, where one household has multiple breadwinners with complex employment responsibilities, and where some parents shuttle their overcommitted children to conflicting activities, fewer people are making time for wake services and funerals. In doing so, they abbreviate their mourning. They choose speed grief. Grief, though, has more command over individuals than they may realize, and a funeral done too quickly can lead into a stage of private life where grief still lurks and demands one's attention.

Pastors do not have much control over the number of stages in a funeral. They can, however, provide counsel. Centuries of experience have given the church a multitiered service that not only accompanies the final journey of the deceased person but helps mourners move through their stages of grief.

On the other hand, American funerals may be evolving. Worldwide, the stages for a funeral change in various lands. When the funeral rites were revised after the Second Vatican Council, the task was towering. Those charged with the revisions realized that the church could surely make some improvements, but it was impossible to account for all the different cultural variations.

The original Latin edition of the OCF orders its contents differently from the current English translation in use in the United States. (The first English translation adhered more closely to the arrangement of contents of the original Latin.) The change was perfectly acceptable to the Vatican because it understood that funeral rites had to be personalized in the various countries and regions. In the United States, the current description of the funeral rites presumes three stages.

In the Latin edition, however, the three-stage process is only one of three options. The other options are funerals in two stages (at the funeral home and the cemetery) and in one stage (at the home of the deceased). The two-stage option does not include a Mass for the dead, but such a Mass may take place at a later time.

The third option, a service in one's home, is unlikely to gain favor in American life. Some Hispanic families, however, observe nine days of prayer in the home of the deceased. Many of their family members and friends consider their attendance at this novena a sacred duty. The Latin edition of the OCF provides options that were removed from the second translation into English in the United States, options that some people have nonetheless unwittingly imitated.

As mentioned above, one of the tragic circumstances that seems to encourage an abbreviated funeral is the death of an infant or a child before birth. The event has so surprised the family, and their grief is so intense, that they want to move through the funeral quickly. Parents especially realize the obligation to bury the dead, but they do not want to prolong this horrific time of grief. Later, some of them regret this choice. They wonder if it would have been more respectful to have fuller services. But they were in deep grief when they needed to make these difficult decisions. Some families choose a shortened funeral for noble reasons.

Other families, perhaps not. Sometimes when I'm visiting with members of the family, they'll tell me, "Mom didn't want a funeral Mass. She just wanted something simple." And in my gut, I know that this cannot be true. I've known their mother. I've witnessed her devotion to the Eucharist. I cannot imagine that she ever expressed disdain for a funeral Mass. I don't presume that the children are lying. Perhaps on one occasion they heard their mother say about her funeral, "Just keep it simple," and in their minds that freed them from having to organize a Mass. If the family does not want a funeral Mass, so be it. The parish can still schedule a Mass for the dead for this deceased Christian. The family may choose to come, or not. But one Mass will be set aside.

The church expects that some Mass will be said for the deceased faithful Christian. The introduction to the OCF, which appears as an appendix in the back of the American edition, says, "Pastoral reasons may on occasion require that a funeral be celebrated in the church without a Mass (which in all cases must, if possible, be celebrated on another day within a reasonable time); in that case a liturgy of the word is prescribed absolutely" (6).

The funeral Mass holds a central place in Catholic piety. The Mass is the sacrament of the sacrifice of Jesus Christ. When we gather, we are present to his self-offering to the Father. We also offer ourselves in sacrifice together with Christ. At a funeral Mass, we are offering the soul of the departed to God, in hopes that the sacrifice of this person's life will be acceptable, as was the death of Jesus. For this reason, the sacramental offering of a funeral Mass is central to the ceremonies surrounding Christian death.

At times a funeral is celebrated without Mass. There are various reasons for this. For example, in parts of the world where priests are scarce, the committal may need to happen before a priest is available for Mass. Pastoral reasons may suggest that this is a more appropriate form of celebration, as when members of the family and other mourners are not Catholic, would not be receiving communion, and would be unfamiliar with the dialogues, postures, and gestures needed for a fitting celebration. Furthermore, there are some days when a funeral Mass is not permitted.

For example, a funeral Mass may not be celebrated on holy days of obligation, Holy Thursday morning and the Paschal Triduum, and the Sundays of Advent, Lent, and Easter (General Instruction on the Roman Missal [GIRM] 380). The introduction to the OCF includes a broader restriction; it says that the funeral Mass is prohibited on solemnities—not just on holy days of obligation (6). However, the Ceremonial of Bishops agrees with the GIRM, and says explicitly that funeral Masses are permitted on solemnities that are not holy days (Appendix III). The same source says that funeral Masses are permitted on the days in the Easter octave, which are solemnities.

This creates inconvenient pastoral situations when a family requests a funeral on one of those restricted days. For example, if they want a funeral on December 8 when it falls on a weekday, the parish can celebrate only the holy day Mass of the Immaculate Conception. The parish may offer the grieving family a funeral without Mass on that day. On holy days, this legislation presumes that Catholics who attend the funeral will return to participate in a holyday Mass, though this is most unlikely. A priest could dispense them from attending the holy day Mass, in accord with canon 1245. The goal of the calendar's legislation is not to create more grief for the family, but to situate the life and death of the Catholic within the church's articles of faith and its liturgical design of their expression. It may inconvenience some of the mourners, but it honors the faith of the deceased Catholic.

The same applies to Sundays. It is possible to celebrate a Catholic funeral on a Sunday, but it needs to be a funeral without Mass. Unless the priest dispenses them, the faithful are expected to participate in the regular parish Mass apart from the funeral. One may discover, however, that cemetery services are not available on Sundays, and the final stage of the funeral may have to be deferred.

Normally the arrangements are simpler. Once they have been made, even the family that feels as if the world has collapsed into chaos may begin to find blessed order and the restoration of peace. The funeral rites help mourners move through their grief and reestablish a sense of normalcy. Nothing will be the same, but life will continue.

Rituals 2

"The Last Rites"

The revision of the sacrament of the anointing of the sick has been one of the greatest successes and one of the greatest failures of the post–Vatican II church. Prior to the council, the sacrament known as "extreme unction" famously constituted the last rites to be requested for a dying Catholic in the moments prior to death. The council successfully changed the meaning of the anointing from a final anointing—the meaning of "extreme unction"—to an anointing that offered potentially healing properties to body and soul. The complete ritual book, *Pastoral Care of the Sick: Rites of Anointing and Viaticum*, treats a variety of circumstances from visiting the sick, offering a repeatable sacramental anointing, to final prayers that feature viaticum (communion for the dying) with its renewal of baptismal promises and plenary indulgence. It also includes prayers for the dying and for the dead that any person may lead.

The change in meaning of the anointing has been largely successful. Catholics in general welcome the anointing of the sick for its healing purposes and willingly present themselves for it as needed, as they should. Yet any priest can tell you stories of people who panicked as soon as he walked into a hospital room, fearing that his presence meant that death was assuredly imminent. In my ministry, one patient screamed at me to get out of her room. On another occasion, family members standing outside a hospital room that I was not visiting watched me walk by. I then overheard one of them say in reference to me, "I sure hope we don't need him." The anointing does not necessarily signal the approach of death, but rather the hopeful prayers of the church in the midst of a serious illness.

Within the popular mind-set remains the belief that a Catholic needs to have a priest just before death. Without a priest, some people believe, eternal salvation is in peril. In pastoral care, any priest would happily be present to lead prayers at this important moment. From the ritual perspective, however, a priest is needed only for confession, anointing, and the apostolic pardon. He may offer confession and anointing earlier, when the person has better health. In the approach of death, another minister may bring communion or lead prayers for the dying. The apostolic pardon can be given only by a priest, but its absence does not extinguish the hope of a merciful judgment from God. Sadly, when a priest offers to visit, some people show their ignorance of the sacrament when they decline an anointing because "it isn't time yet."

Priests all get requests for "the last rites," but there is no section of *Pastoral Care of the Sick* with that title. What priests offer depends on what the person has received so far. Even the final prayers do not absolutely demand the presence of a priest.

Below is a chart to help visualize the various rites that the church offers to those who are sick and dying. All of these are found or referenced in the volume *Pastoral Care of the Sick: Rites of Anointing and Viaticum.*

SERVICE	RECIPIENT	MINISTER
Visiting the Sick	Any sick person	Anyone
Communion	Any sick person eligible and capable	Communion minister
Anointing	Reality or possibility of serious illness	Priest
Reconciliation	Any eligible sick person	Priest
Viaticum	One who is dying	Communion minister
Prayers for the dying	One who is dying	Anyone
Prayers for the dead	One who has died	Anyone

Anyone may visit any person who is sick, using the appropriate prayers and readings in the volume.

An extraordinary minister of Holy Communion may bring communion to any sick person who is eligible for communion in the Catholic Church and is physically able to swallow.

Only a priest may administer the sacrament of the anointing of the sick, which is offered to those who have the reality or the possibility of serious illness.

Only a priest may offer the sacrament of reconciliation, and any eligible person—sick or healthy—may confess.

Any extraordinary minister of Holy Communion may bring Viaticum to a person who is dying. Even the Order for the Commissioning of Extraordinary Ministers of Holy Communion from the *Book of Blessings* assigns this responsibility (1875).

Anyone may lead the prayers for the dying and the prayers for the dead from *Pastoral Care of the Sick*. These collections of prayers do not involve a sacrament and do not require an ordained minister to lead them.

Many people assume that they need a priest for the last rites, but it depends on which last rites they mean. If it is the church's officials prayers for the dying, anyone may lead them, even a member of the family.

The Liturgical Environment

Decorations at the church will form a liturgical environment for the funeral rites. Many parishes may already have seasonal decorations in place: a wreath and purple appointments during Advent, poinsettias and a tree for Christmas, a spare use of purple elements for Lent, lilies for Easter, and greenery for Ordinary Time. These need not be rearranged for a funeral Mass, even though this ritual Mass displaces the regular liturgical celebration. A funeral takes place within a certain time of year, and the decorations inside and outside the church may reflect it. These may even help mourners call to mind the season of year when they observed the funeral.

Flowers often arrive in abundance for a funeral. Friends of the deceased, especially those who cannot be physically present, may send floral arrangements as a sign of love. Some obituaries carry a notice requesting no flowers, but it will not stop some people from sending them anyway.

In Catholic churches, flowers may be arranged around the altar, but not on top of it. They may be used in moderation during Advent and not at all during Lent (GIRM 305). Nonetheless, flowers will probably arrive for a funeral, even in Lent.

Many parish ministers develop plans for the placement of flowers at a funeral. Most funeral directors want to know what these are and to abide by them. Sometimes funeral home employees do not ask; they mean well, but they inadvertently place flower arrangements where they may pose an obstacle to the flow of the liturgy. Flowers should not obstruct access to the sanctuary or the processional paths to the ambo. Nor should they block anyone's view of the activities taking place during the funeral. Although the sanctuary of every Catholic Church follows certain conventions, each is unique, and ministers will have to consider the most favorable array of flowers.

Some families may want to place photos and other mementos of the deceased in a significant place. For these, a special table could be set before the liturgy begins. As with flowers, the table should not obstruct the assembly's view of the liturgical actions, nor sit directly in front of the altar. Sometimes a position near a communion station works well, or near the entrance to the building. Photos should not be placed on top of the coffin. The coffin is not a shelf. Christian symbols may be placed there, as will be seen, but other remembrances of the deceased belong in a separate place.

If the body has been cremated, the ashes should be placed in a dignified container. If the crematorium returned the remains to the family in a fragile box, it may be placed inside a more suitable vessel. In this way the cremated remains can be treated with the same dignity accorded a body. A parish may obtain a reusable vessel for such purposes. Some funeral homes offer an ark for transporting the cremated remains. The urn sits inside a wooden or metal box with walls of glass, supported by horizontal poles for pallbearers to hold.

Christian symbols may be placed upon the coffin when it first arrives at the church; for example, a Book of the Gospels, a Bible, or a cross (OCF 38, 163). If so, before the liturgy begins, these may be arranged close at hand in the part of the church where the action will take place.

Appropriate vestments for priests and deacons should also be selected. In the United States these may be white, purple, or black in color. In the United States the black vestments required prior to the Second Vatican Council were almost universally replaced with white ones after the council. This contributed to the shift in moods accompanying the liturgical celebration of funerals. Some priests, however, prefer to wear purple or black on the assumption that the presidential prayers are more hopeful than celebratory, and that even the vestments may acknowledge the real grief of mourners. If a priest wears black and does not explain why, some Catholic mourners may assume that he extends no hope of eternal life. When a pope dies, the concelebrating priests wear red, a sign that he was the successor of Peter the Apostle; red is the vestment color for the liturgical days that honor Peter and the other martyrs.

Pallbearers add to the ceremony and have traditional responsibilities of accompanying the coffin from the hearse to the church and back again. They often join in the processions at the beginning and end of the funeral Mass. At the cemetery they may help carry the coffin to its place of committal. In the case of cremation, one or more persons could be designated to carry the remains with dignity. Six is the traditional number of pallbearers, probably because of the number of handles on a coffin, but the Catholic Church has no rule pertaining to the number of them. A grieving family could request greater or fewer than six. Nor is there any rule requiring that pallbearers be male. Women may participate in addition to or in replacement of men. The OCF assigns virtually no liturgical responsibility to pallbearers. Funeral directors, more familiar with the process of rolling a coffin, generally make the necessary adjustments for its proper placement once the pallbearers have fulfilled their task.

If the vigil for the deceased is taking place in the church immediately before the funeral Mass, the coffin will be carried from the hearse inside the church before the mourners arrive. Funeral home employees usually perform this action without the pallbearers. However, conscientious pallbearers could set the time aside to perform this function, even though it will be out of view of almost every other mourner.

Veterans of war deserve the gratitude and respect of the community. Many of them, proud to have served their country, want the national flag close to their remains. A flag may drape the coffin for its arrival at the church and cemetery; however, inside the church the funeral pall will replace the flag. The American edition of the OCF says strongly that national flags "have no place" in the funeral liturgy (38). They are to be removed when the coffin arrives and may be replaced when it leaves (132). Still, if a table has been established for photos and other mementos of the deceased, a folded national flag would fittingly rest there. If the parish usually has a national flag on display inside the church, it need not be removed for a funeral.

A funeral pall covers every coffin during mass, though it is omitted in the case of cremation (OCFa 434), presumably because it would be too large. Furthermore, the pall symbolizes the baptismal garment that clothed the body, and there is nothing to be clothed after cremation. A typical parish has its own pall that is used for every funeral. Some palls were handmade by a member of the community; others purchased from national suppliers. Some palls are designed to match the particular white vesture worn by the priest at a funeral Mass. Usually the same pall covers every body from oldest to youngest, most active to least, no matter the identity of the deceased. A white garment recalls one's baptism, and it is the uniform of those who dwell in the kingdom of heaven.

White garments appear in several key passages of the New Testament. At the transfiguration, Jesus' garments became white (Matt 17:2; Mark 9:3; Luke 9:29). When mourners entered Jesus' tomb, they found a man dressed in white announcing the resurrection (Mark 16:5). At Jesus' final appearance to his followers, his garments were as white as snow (Matt 28:3). At the ascension, two men in white address the apostles (Acts 1:10). White is the color of the garments worn by those in heaven in the book of Revelation (3:4; 3:5; 4:4; 6:11; 7:9, 13; and 19:14). The white garment is given at the time of baptism as an anticipation of the garment the person hopes to wear in heaven. The priest or deacon presenting the garment at baptism says to the newly baptized that it symbolizes Christian dignity. "Bring that dignity unstained into the everlasting life of heaven" (Rite of Baptism for Children 63). That is the garment that covers the coffin, a reminder of baptism past, a promise of future glory for those whom Christ redeems.

The Wake

The Vigil for the Deceased

The first of the three traditional stages is the vigil for the deceased, commonly called the wake service. Catholics generally expect it to take place in a funeral home. Many Catholics expect someone, preferably a priest, to lead a rosary. The time before or after the vigil provides an occasion and setting for friends to share condolences with the grieving family.

For this occasion, the OCF has designed a liturgy, not a devotional exercise. People may gather at church, at the funeral home, or in the home of the deceased. A priest, deacon, or layperson leads the service, which includes biblical readings and prayers. Seeing a lay leader of prayer is still somewhat rare, but having a lay leader can affirm the skills of a respected member of the staff or of the parish community, while allowing the priest greater control over his other plans during the week. There are some ceremonies for which the liturgy does not demand the presence of a priest, and this is one of them.

> In my first weeks as pastor of one parish, I remember leading the vigil for the deceased exactly as the OCF calls for it. We celebrated it in church. I used ministers to provide music, proclaim readings, and lead the litany. I thought it went rather well, considering that this community had probably never experienced a vigil service like this. As I walked out, I was confident that I had set a strong precedent for the future celebration of this liturgy. Immediately afterward, though, some of my new parishioners, aiming to set me straight, cornered me and said, "You did it wrong. You didn't say the rosary."

Because the liturgy envisions a chair, an ambo, and singing, the church makes a suitable location. Musical instruments occupy their space, and people can find participation aids at their seats. The sanctuary is clearly defined. The parish is accustomed to the needs for parking and hospitality. Some newer churches are designed with a vigil service in mind—including a spacious area where a coffin may be placed and where mourners may gather.

Some funeral directors may prefer to have the vigil for the deceased in their own chapel. They are used to the routine, and they have restrooms, drinking fountains, and adequate parking. Hosting the vigil service at the funeral home brings people onto the property to meet the staff, and it may make them think about their own funeral arrangements. On other occasions a funeral director may be happy to have the service at the church because it allows more flexibility for other grieving families who want a visitation on the same night. This becomes more important when a large number of mourners is expected at one service.

Choosing the parish church for the location poses a couple of practical dilemmas. One pertains to the funeral pall. The OCF calls for it to be placed on the coffin when it first arrives at the church, which would be at the vigil (82–86). However, it will then have to be removed immediately if people intend to view the deceased, which is one of the main reasons that the body is present. Consequently it is extremely rare for the pall to be placed on the coffin when it arrives at the church for the vigil. Often the funeral directors bring the remains of the deceased to church before anyone arrives and arrange the area for the viewing before there is any liturgical action. However, if a minister is available when the coffin and family arrive at the church, a brief prayer service could take place among them. If because of the tragic nature of the person's death the coffin will be closed for the vigil, then placing the pall when the body enters the church poses fewer problems. Otherwise, covering the coffin with the pall at the beginning of the vigil remains impractical.

Second, the parish, the family, and the funeral home have to reach a decision about the placement of the coffin overnight. If it is to be transported back to the funeral home, there may be an extra expense. If it is to remain in the church, it probably does not have professional overnight surveillance—though mourners may wish to hold an all-night vigil. In some cases an organization such as the Knights of Columbus provide this service. Nonetheless, good conversation and planning can resolve these questions. Especially for those who were active in the parish church, holding the vigil there will draw mourners to the central location of faith that can house the entirety of the person's life and values. But people should take all the necessary precautions.

Most people, however, expect that the vigil will take place at the funeral home, and many funeral homes house a nondenominational prayer room. Such a room can be furnished with a crucifix and a kneeler, making them look Catholic for the sake of the vigil, although the OCF makes no such requirements. They are the devotional furnishings one anticipates when the main prayer taking place in the room is the rosary.

The vigil may take place in the home of the deceased, a custom observed in some ethnic groups. If mourners are many, the constricted space will change the feel of liturgical prayer. The leader may find it hard to focus everyone's attention, or, more positively, the close quarters may draw people even more deeply into the service of prayer.

The vigil has a straightforward structure. Although rubrics do not indicate changes of posture, it would be appropriate for all to stand at the beginning if they are able. If the service is taking place in the home of the deceased, this may prove more difficult. But normally, having everyone stand will signal the start of formal prayer.

The minister greets the people using one of the suggested formulas (OCF 69). All these examples presume that the minister is an ordained priest or deacon, to whom the response "And with your spirit" is given. However, similar words of greeting may be used, and these would be especially appropriate for a lay presider. For example, in *Sunday Celebrations in the Absence of a Priest*, the greeting that opens a celebration of the Liturgy of the Word has the deacon or lay leader say, "Grace and peace to you from God our Father and from the Lord Jesus Christ. Blessed be God for ever." To which all respond, "Blessed be God for ever" (188).

Then a song is sung (OCF 70). The OCF provides no specific suggestions, but those familiar with planning music for funerals will find here another opportunity to sing something that will acknowledge grief, affirm faith, and offer hope.

The minister invites those gathered to pray (71). A time of silent prayer follows, and then the minister offers an opening prayer for the liturgy (72). Two samples are given, but there are a great many more in the later pages of the OCF. Careful planning will help the minister select one that especially fits the circumstance.

The Liturgy of the Word follows. It resembles the presentation of the readings that one expects at a weekday Mass. People may be seated to hear the first reading followed by a responsorial psalm (73–75). It would be appropriate for them to stand for the gospel. The service does not envision a second reading before the gospel (59), probably because this is not the main celebration, which will follow the next day. Although the funeral Mass does not require three readings, it permits them.

Members of the family or friends may help proclaim the readings, preferably if they have experience as readers at church. If a priest or deacon is leading this service, he may give a homily (77). This may prove redundant if the same minister is going to preach at the funeral Mass. The prayer of intercession follows, beginning with a litany (78). An assisting minister may read the intentions, either the same person who proclaimed the first reading or a different one.

I find that using other ministers to help with the reading and this litany can engage the entire assembly even more. If I am the only one performing all the parts of this service, it may leave people watching, rather than participating. Having a cantor, reader, or assisting minister along can keep interest and participation alive.

The presiding minister then leads all in the Lord's Prayer, which concludes the intercessions (79). At Mass, intercessions such as these conclude with a prayer by the priest, but here it is the Lord's Prayer that draws them to a close. The same sequence happens at Morning and Evening Prayer in the Liturgy of the Hours. The prayer that comes next is the concluding prayer to the entire celebration.

When that prayer is over, "a member or friend of the family may speak in remembrance of the deceased" (80). A similar rubric appears in the funeral Mass. Thus the OCF presents two opportunities for a mourner to speak. The original Latin does not provide such an opportunity at the vigil for the deceased, though it does for the funeral Mass. Many have found that the vigil makes a better setting for such reflections, which are unpredictable in length and content.

The concluding rite is a blessing (81). The minister may trace the sign of the cross on the forehead of the deceased or make some other gesture. The minister leads the people in a familiar dialogue unique to funerals:

Minister: Eternal rest grant unto him (her), O Lord.

People: And let perpetual light shine upon him (her).

Minister: May he (she) rest in peace.

People: Amen.

Minister: May his (her) soul and the souls of all the faithful
departed, through the mercy of God, rest in peace.

People: Amen.

Every Catholic should learn this dialogue. It is part of the tradition for burying the dead.

At times I have led this dialogue only to discover that people do not know the responses. It may help to have a participation aid available for the people, at least in some circumstances, so that they can find assurance in the comforting words of peace. Another solution is to be sure that an assisting minister knows the responses and can prompt the people. Least desirable is for the presider to lead and respond to the dialogue. It then ceases to be a dialogue.

The service closes with a prayer of blessing and a song or a period of silence.

In practice, the vigil could either begin or conclude the period of visitation. Some like it at the beginning to set the tone for what follows. Others like it at the end to gather people in prayer and send them on their way.

This same service can be conducted in the presence of cremated remains, though without the white pall, and obviously without the minister signing the forehead of the deceased.

The vigil for the deceased, which is designed without the recitation of the rosary, appropriately gathers all mourners. Those unfamiliar with the rosary can still hear readings and prayers that proclaim Christian hope. In a gathering that may be both ecumenical and interreligious, the vigil offers care for the mourners as well.

Some wonder if the vigil for the deceased could include a rosary.
I think it is better to keep the two prayers separate. Perhaps
someone from the family could lead a rosary at the beginning
of the visitation, and then a minister from the parish could lead
the vigil at the end. If a blending is preferred, it makes some
liturgical sense to have the rosary replace the litany and Lord's
Prayer (OCF 94–95).

Others may insist on the rosary but agree to include some
aspects of the vigil. I may do this in the interests of peace; after
all, this liturgy is somewhat flexible, and the tradition behind
the rosary is strong. But at a bare minimum, I think that some
Scripture should be proclaimed, probably before the rosary
begins. That would set the devotional prayer as an echo to the
word of God.

There is no rule governing the mysteries to be prayed. Some
choose the Sorrowful Mysteries, in order to place the death of
this Christian within the context of the death of Christ. Others
prefer the Glorious Mysteries, which begin with the hope of
resurrection. I know one priest who uses the last two Sorrowful
Mysteries concerning the cross, and the first three of the Glorious
Mysteries—from the resurrection to the descent of the Spirit.
This pulls together several elements of the paschal mystery.

Some ethnic groups see the wake as an occasion for men to visit
and smoke and for women to prepare a meal. Although grief
accompanies any death, so does socialization in different forms.
Such gender distinctions have become offensive in much of the
American culture.

Liturgy of the Hours

As an alternative to the vigil service, mourners may pray part
of the Liturgy of the Hours for the dead (OCF 54). Although the
Second Vatican Council hoped that the revision of the Liturgy of
the Hours and its communal celebration would take root even

among laypeople in parishes, this has not in fact become wide-spread. Many Catholics are unfamiliar with this liturgical prayer of the church. Still, if participation aids have been developed, people can follow them without much difficulty.

From the Liturgy of the Hours the obvious choices for an evening vigil would be Evening Prayer or even the Office of Readings. If the main funeral liturgy takes place in the evening, Morning Prayer for the dead could be prayed the following day before going to the place of interment (OCF 348).

In the rare instances where mourners wish to keep an all-night vigil, various common liturgical prayers could distribute themselves throughout the night: Evening Prayer, the Office of Readings, or Night Prayer. Apart from convents and monasteries, though, this is probably rare.

Many families do not want a vigil service at all. They simply allow a period of visitation before the funeral Mass begins. In most cases, such a visitation does not include a rosary or the liturgical vigil. It could, but families choosing to eliminate a gathering the night before the funeral Mass are usually eliminating a separate time of public prayer as well. One practical advantage of the vigil for the deceased is that it gives friends two options for paying their respects. But in some cases, they receive only one opportunity to come.

Related Rites and Prayers

The church offers a variety of other rites and prayers that may be appropriate, depending on the circumstances of the death and on the mourners. These rites are Prayers after Death, Gathering in the Presence of the Body, and Transfer of the Body to the Church or to the Place of Committal.

Prayers after Death may be fittingly offered shortly after the moment of death, perhaps even before the funeral directors have removed the body from its place (OCF 104–8). The minister, who may be a layperson, invites all to pray in silence. The minister or another person then reads a passage from Scripture. The minister leads all in the Lord's Prayer, and then offers concluding prayers—one oration for the deceased and another for the mourners. The minister leads those present in the funeral dialogue ("Eternal rest grant. . . .") and offers a blessing. The service is brief, but well focused on the moment and on the raw emotions at hand. In parishes, a priest is not always available for such occasions, but whoever goes to minister to the mourners in these moments after death may choose to lead these prayers from the OCF or those from *Pastoral Care of the Sick.*

Gathering in the Presence of the Body is another short prayer service that may be done in a slightly different circumstance (OCF 112–18). Perhaps a little later after death—at the funeral home, for example—the immediate family or a small group of mourners gather in the presence of the one who has died. The minister leads those gathered in the sign of the cross. Someone reads a passage from Scripture. All pray in silence. The minister may sprinkle the body with blessed water. A psalm is then prayed. If one of those present is a reader at Mass familiar with the structure of a responsorial, that person may lead the psalm. The minister invites all to offer the Lord's Prayer. After a concluding prayer, the minister may sign the forehead of the deceased, or make some other gesture. The minister leads the dialogue ("Eternal rest grant. . . .") and says a blessing. Often when family members arrive at the funeral home to see the body for the first time in the coffin, they naturally grow silent and may appreciate some direction. A minister leading this service can help them.

In the case of cremation, this service could be performed at the crematorium just before the body enters the chamber. Or during or immediately after cremation, a minister could lead the service without making the references to the body, such as 114c, or the final optional signing of the forehead.

Transfer of the Body to the Church or the Place of Committal is the third of the related rites (OCF 121–26). As its title suggests, it precedes a procession. Logistically it is hard for people in procession to recite prayers together, but they could offer these prayers before beginning their journey.

The minister introduces the service. Someone reads a passage from Scripture. The minister leads the mourners in a litany, followed by the Lord's Prayer. The minister says a concluding prayer and invites all to silence to prepare for the procession. The minister invites all to join the procession. During the procession, psalms may be sung or recited, such as Psalm 122, "I rejoiced when I heard them say: let us go to the house of the Lord." This may prove difficult in lengthy processions, but the beautiful concept of praying during the procession deserves further thought.

Wailing is an acceptable—and expected—form of grief in some cultures. Sometimes the processions to and from the church are marked by people—usually women—who wail loudly, cry real tears, clutch the coffin, and may require physical support in the midst of their crying. Some families hire professional wailers. The custom is regarded as an acceptable expression of grief in some cultures; in fact, its absence may suggest that the family really is not grieving the death at all.

The Funeral Mass

Introductory Rites

The main funeral liturgy is the Mass. As explained above, if for some reason Mass cannot be celebrated as part of the funeral, it should be celebrated on a later day, even if the closest members of the family are unable to participate.

The paschal candle may be placed near the position where the coffin will rest after the procession (162). Although this is not required, it is broadly practiced in the United States. The candle should be placed where its association with the coffin is clear, in order to proclaim the mystery of resurrection promised to the faithful followers of Christ. Yet it should not be placed where it may obstruct the view of mourners participating in the mass.

In the early days of the post–Vatican II revisions, during the entrance procession of a funeral, ministers in some parishes carried the paschal candle in place of the processional cross. This option does not appear in the OCF, probably because the procession with the paschal candle is unique to the Easter Vigil, and the cross makes a more fitting symbol of death and the hope of resurrection. The processional cross need not have the image of the crucified Christ if such an image is permanently displayed in the church.

Traditionally, the funeral Mass takes place in the morning. It becomes the event of focus for the mourners. They wake up, go to church, pray the mass, go to the cemetery, and have the rest of the day to reflect on these activities. However, some are choosing an evening funeral Mass. In this case, the visitation precedes the funeral Mass. Depending on the length of the visitation, it could begin with the vigil for the deceased and conclude with the funeral Mass. But many families will simply choose to omit the vigil, allow the visitation to fill the time, and conclude with the funeral Mass.

The funeral Mass begins with the introductory rites, when the body is received at the door of the church. Usually the family has gathered at the funeral home and has arrived in their cars and the vehicles rented for the occasion.

In many cases, however, the visitation has taken place inside the church during the hours immediately preceding the funeral Mass. The coffin is already inside the building, usually near the place where it will rest during the funeral Mass. In this case, funeral directors often ask if the coffin should be brought back to the door of the church, or if the liturgy should begin where it already is. Similarly, they ask if the family members who have been inside the church should now leave their pews and go back to the door for the opening rites. The rubrics do not envision the possibility of a visitation in church before the funeral Mass, so priests hold different opinions about what to do. Many priests feel that it is artificial to roll the coffin back to the door and create an entrance procession as if the body had never been inside. The simpler solution is to leave the coffin in place and to begin as other masses begin—with a procession of the ministers up the aisle, followed by the opening rites from the sanctuary. On the other hand, the priest and the ministers are probably visible in the church's nave for some time before a funeral Mass begins; when they go to the door for the entrance procession, no one considers it artificial. Would not the same apply to the remains of the deceased? The procession including the family may also signal a shift in purpose as they accompany their deceased relative one last time into the place of worship.

If the funeral Mass takes place apart from the visitation, the family usually arrives together with the remains of the deceased. The OCF envisions that mourners will follow the coffin into the church after the opening rites, so upon arrival they gather somewhere near the front door. The OCF calls this group "the mourners" (162), without explaining further if they are family or close friends, few or great in number. Sometimes a limited amount of space available by the door of the church, or a circumstance such as inclement weather, will suggest that the mourners enter the building and take their places for Mass upon their arrival. However, the liturgy envisions that they have gathered near the coffin where they will participate in the opening rites.

Some priests prefer to have the family take their places in pews regardless of the size of the narthex and the weather. They think that the opening rites make more sense further up the middle aisle, closer to the sanctuary. That way everyone in church is close to the action, and visibility is increased. After all, OCF 162 envisions that "the mourners" are going to be near the coffin for this opening ceremony. The OCF, however, calls for this opening ceremony to take place near the door because something significant is happening as the remains of the deceased enter the church for the last time. Honor is bestowed near the door before the coffin approaches the sanctuary. Even though those seated in front of the church may be far from this initial action, those seated in the back will be drawn into the ceremony more than usual. If the ceremony is to begin out of view of guests who are already in their places, the song leader or deacon would appropriately invite them to stand and turn so that they may participate more actively.

The priest goes to the door of the church (159). The OCF says nothing about the sign of the cross that usually begins a Mass. Is the priest to omit it because of the unusual nature of this rite? Or does the OCF presume that the priest knows he should begin Mass in the usual way? It is likely that he is expected to start in the usual way with the sign of the cross to signal the beginning of the service. OCF 165 says that the Liturgy of the Word comes "after the introductory rites," which seems to imply the usual rites, except where those unique to funerals are clearly noted.

The priest sprinkles the coffin with blessed water while reciting a text recalling the waters of baptism (160). The pall may be placed on the coffin at this time (161). This is optional, although one sees it commonly in the United States. The rubric suggests that family members, friends, or the priest place the pall. In practice, the funeral directors sometimes step in to perform this action, even though the rubric does not list them among the people who may place the pall. Regardless, they have done it many times, family members and friends have not, and the priest has to manage his copy of the OCF, a sprinkler, and a bucket. Even so, the action is not a difficult one, and through it families can make a final loving act of placing clothing over the body of the deceased. Funeral home employees could appropriately give direction without being overzealous.

As mentioned above, in the case of cremation, the placing of the pall is omitted (OCFa 434).

As in any Mass, incense may be used in the entrance procession. Incense will be used near the end of the service. Using it at other times (entrance, gospel procession, preparation of the gifts, and eucharistic prayer) can lend solemnity to the entire funeral Mass. At the entrance, incense leads the procession into the church, even ahead of the cross.

Servers or other helpers may need to carry several items in this procession: the incense and boat if the priest is going to use them when he reaches the sanctuary, the OCF itself unless the priest keeps a second copy at the chair, and holy water if he intends to sprinkle during the final commendation.

The priest and the ministers all precede the coffin and the mourners. As in weddings, the priest is not the last one in the procession. The bride and groom, who administer the sacrament to each other, come last in the wedding procession, and at funerals, the mourners accompany the coffin or the urn containing the cremated remains, as if the deceased is celebrating the eucharistic sacrifice one last time, actively offering his or her soul to the care of God. This arrangement also offers the practical advantage of getting the ministers into the sanctuary without having to slide past the coffin after it has been placed in the center aisle.

Out of habit, mourners often enter the pew and sit down, even though the entrance song is being sung. An usher, sacristan, deacon, or funeral director could help by quietly informing mourners as they take their place to remain standing.

The English edition of the OCF in the United States gives no instructions for the arrangement of the coffin in the aisle. The original Latin, however, says that, if appropriate, the traditional custom is retained: the deceased assumes his or her usual position in the assembly of the faithful. A deceased member of the faithful faces the altar, and a deceased sacred minister faces the people (*Ordo Exsequiarum* [OE] 38). The rubric also appears in the Ceremonial of Bishops (823). For this reason, a coffin is usually brought up the aisle feet first.

A symbol such as the Book of the Gospels, a Bible, or a cross may be carried in procession and then placed upon the coffin in silence or as the minister offers an explanatory text (OCF 163, 400). There should be only one object, and it should be a symbol of the Christian life, not an otherwise biographical commentary on the interests and pastimes of the deceased. The placement of symbols here treats the coffin as if it were an altar, the other object in the church upon which a cross or Book of the Gospels may rest. One theme of the Catholic funeral ceremony is that deceased Christians make an offering of their lives to God, just as Jesus offered his life on the cross. The coffin in the aisle carries some resemblance to the altar of sacrifice in the sanctuary.

The rubric envisions that the object is carried in procession and placed upon the coffin once it has reached its place for the Mass. This lends dignity to the object, puts the ceremonial action inside the church nearer to the sanctuary, and resolves the practical concern that it could fall to the ground en route.

At a Catholic funeral a funeral director usually places a cross on the coffin immediately after it has been covered with the pall near the door of the church. Sometimes this cross is provided by the funeral home; other times it is supplied by the family. This gesture fits within the vision of OCF 163, though it more properly belongs at the end of the procession. Surprisingly, placing a cross on the coffin is not required at a Catholic funeral, even though it is quite common, and it is not the only symbolic object that may occupy that space.

Some priests do not want the funeral directors to be visible during the ceremony. They want pallbearers and family members to move the coffin into position. Some priests hold a cynical view that employees of the funeral home are mercenaries, performing their duties in order to be paid, and putting themselves on view in hopes of attracting more business. However, funeral directors usually get into this business with a desire to serve others and to make a difference in society. The ideal funeral employees are those who actually participate in the liturgy, taking a pew, singing the hymns, joining in the responses, and listening to the Scriptures. They can pray and work diligently, respectfully, and unnoticeably. They can offer a nearly diaconal assistance so that the priest can focus on his prayer.

The priest offers the opening prayer (the collect) after reverencing the altar (OCF 164). The penitential rite and Gloria are omitted. The OCF provides a wide variety of opening prayers to cover particular circumstances of death. These treat differences of age, marital status, church involvement, and the cause of death (398). These were composed at a time when the Vatican encouraged the writing of some prayers directly within the vernacular languages. They offer a good example of an attempt to express in prayer the genius of the English language, its rhythms, and its imagery. The Roman Missal has a collection of presidential prayers amid its Masses for the Dead. The collects there may be used as the opening prayer of the funeral Mass. These are divided among those that may be offered during or outside of Easter Time. The Easter collect builds upon the faith in the resurrection celebrated at that time of year. Until such time as the Vatican approves a revised English translation of the entire OCF, priests may choose one of these collects or one from the additional opening prayers in the OCF.

Liturgy of the Word

The readings are proclaimed as on a weekday or a Sunday. Either two or three readings are appropriate. They follow the usual rules for selection. The first reading usually comes from the Old Testament; during Easter Time, however, it more fittingly draws from Acts of the Apostles or the book of Revelation. If there will be only two readings, the first reading may come from one of the New Testament letters. A responsorial psalm comes next. If there are three readings, the passage from a New Testament letter follows the psalm. The gospel acclamation introduces the procession and proclamation of the gospel, which is always the final reading.

Incense, which has been prepared for the end of the celebration, may be used at the proclamation of the gospel as well, according to the usual custom.

> I've put in the Toolbox section of this book (pp. 75–96) a commentary on each of the readings proposed in the Lectionary for Masses for the Dead. It includes a summary of Catholic teaching and circumstances for which the reading may be appropriate. I've also given you a collection of keywords found in the readings from this section of the Lectionary. These may help you select the best readings for a particular funeral.

The priest or deacon preaches the homily. The rubric is strong: A brief homily is *always* given (OCF 27). The only other homily that is required is at the Easter Vigil. On that occasion, even if brief, the homily "is not to be omitted" (See The Easter Vigil in the Holy Night 36 in *The Roman Missal*).

Many preachers rely on a few comforting thoughts that they repeat for each funeral. Pastoral demands and the challenge of creativity make it hard for them to compose something new every time. The time spent with the family, however, can inspire a homilist to preach specifically to the case at hand.

Here are a few tips that I have learned:

• Be specific, not generic. Do the hard work of preparing a new homily for each funeral. A Christian has died. He or she deserves to be treated with respect.

• Share your experience of the deceased person if you can. I find that even a single story about a conversation I had with the person, or something I learned from others, will relax people and stir up their own memories.

• Do not say these four words out loud in public in reference to your relationship with the deceased person: "I never knew N." Even if that is true, those words can sound hurtful to mourners. Some preachers like to admit that they never knew the person because it makes them feel better about speaking on this occasion. However, it almost never makes the mourners feel better. They will wonder, "Well, why didn't he get to know N.?" We priests command a significant role in religious leadership. Although it is not fair or true, people associate our knowledge of a deceased person with God's knowledge of that person. Mourners blurring this distinction may feel fear or anger, as if we are blaming the deceased for not getting to know us, or that our lack of contact implies God's lack of contact as well.

• Don't canonize the person. When we greet family members after death, it is tempting to say, "He's in a better place"; "His suffering is over"; "She is now in the loving arms of her husband again"; "She can watch over us now." While aiming to console, we are assuming the role of Jesus Christ, whose job is to come to judge the living and the dead. We may think that the deceased person has gone to heaven, but we cannot know this. This is probably why the OCF says that the homily should never be any kind of eulogy (27). I don't think it means to exclude biographical statements about the deceased, or even the mention of their virtues. The OCF simply does not want you to proclaim that eternal life has now come. As you'll see in the prayers over the offerings, these all assume that the

> deceased is a sinner, and our role is not to proclaim otherwise,
> but to pray accordingly.

The Universal Prayer

As at any mass, the universal prayer invites the priestly people
of God to exercise their responsibility and pray for the needs of
the church and the world. The OCF calls this the "general intercessions" (167). They are commonly called the prayer of the faithful.
The Missal no longer uses the expression "general intercessions,"
favoring instead "universal prayer." The prayer is not general,
but universal in its scope.

Samples are included in the OCF, and in the Missal's fifth appendix, example 11. Other petitions may be added or substituted.
If the conversation with the family has uncovered some particular
themes, these could appear in the petitions. Parish life is so busy
that ministers often repeat the same petitions from funeral to
funeral. But these prayers can help personalize the funeral. Someone has to prepare these, which represents more work, but they
can be more effective when written with a precise purpose.

A family member or another mourner may read the petitions.
The same rules apply as to the one who may proclaim a reading.
It helps the liturgy if someone familiar with reading petitions steps
forward. People unfamiliar with this part of the mass may not
know when to leave their place, how to reverence the altar, how
to use the microphone, or the basic structure of the prayers. These
can be taught, but not everyone will remember the instructions.
It also creates the embarrassing possibility that a mourner standing up in public so soon after the death of a loved one may suc-
cumb to grief and become incapable of completing the task.

The Liturgy of the Eucharist

A procession of the gifts may take place. This is not required at
any Mass, but it is always a good idea. At funerals the procession
may involve additional family members or mourners.

To be avoided is the carrying of extraneous items in this procession. It should include bread and wine. It normally does not include a cruet of water (GIRM 73), though it may (GIRM 118c). Water is not as important to the nature of this procession as the other elements are. Someone may bring forward the financial offerings for the church or the poor, although these are rarely collected at a funeral. If the obituary, however, recommended that donations be awarded to a charity, some indication of those gifts could be included in the procession. The procession is not the place for biographical mementos: insignia of favorite sports teams, awards conferred at work, articles of clothing, or household items. Some people encourage children to carry roses in procession and place them in a vase in front of the altar. This has the advantage of involving more people in one element of the liturgy, but if the ultimate purpose of this action is decorative, it has no place at this time. The point of the procession of gifts is to bring forward the offerings for sacrifice, not to carry up environmental elements that could be set in place before the liturgy begins or possessions that will be returned to the family when the liturgy ends. No other symbol of the person's life has greater importance than the person's body, which is being offered to God at this time, never to return again.

Incense may be used for the preparation of the gifts, as usual. If so, when the deacon or server incenses the congregation, the body of the deceased will naturally be included in the offering. At this time of the Mass, the community prays that God will be pleased with the offering of their lives. The incensation of the bread, wine, priest, and people accompanies these prayers in hopes that God will be pleased by the sweet aroma of the sacrifices on and around the altar.

The prayer over the offerings brings these intentions to the fore. The several options presented in the Missal all pray that God will find the offering of the life of the deceased Christian favorable. One of these orations prays that the deceased will find God to be a merciful judge. Another prays that any sin committed may be forgiven. Still another asks God to wash away the sins of the deceased. These prayers take a humble, realistic approach to assessing the moral life of the deceased and the seriousness of God's judgment. Those who offer glib words of consolation in conversation with the family or in the funeral homily will find themselves at odds with these prayers. As mentioned above, the Vatican's document on children who die before baptism failed to state unequivocally that they are granted eternal life. If the church cannot confidently proclaim salvation even of innocent babes at their untimely death, ministers should be cautious about saying as much for anyone else among the deceased.

Admittedly, the introduction to the final commendation states confidently concerning the deceased, "One day we shall joyfully greet him/her again" (171A), and of the congregation, "the mercy of God will gather us together again in the joy of his kingdom" (171B). The English translation differs slightly from the Latin original, which views both of these statements as expressions of hope more than declarations of certainty. Furthermore, these invitations appeared first in the post–Vatican II funeral liturgy and do not enjoy the more time-tested and formal tradition of the presidential prayers of a funeral Mass.

The Eucharistic Prayer

Of the various eucharistic prayers in the Roman Missal, the most appropriate ones for a funeral are I, II, and III. Eucharistic Prayer IV has a preface that cannot be replaced, so using it means that one of the prefaces proper to a Mass for the Dead cannot be proclaimed. The ones for masses of reconciliation, children, and various needs and occasions are probably not as appropriate because they all have other themes and assemblies in mind.

The first preface in the Missal is the one from the pre–Vatican II Mass for the Dead. The other four are recent compositions based on other ancient prefaces and some biblical passages. They each carry titles that summarize their contents, in order to help the priest make a choice for the funeral at hand. Although connections between the prefaces and the particular deceased person may not be as clear as the connections between the same person and the

Scripture readings, making a deliberate choice of one preface over another will help the priest proclaim it with more meaning.

Eucharistic Prayer I includes a space where the names of individuals among the dead may be read aloud. At a funeral, it would be appropriate for the priest to pronounce the name of the deceased person. Eucharistic Prayers II and III have embolisms, prayers that expand a text. These were composed for funerals or other Masses for the Dead. They are also based on biblical passages, and help draw the faithful into the eucharistic prayer more directly. Often it seems as though the church gets quieter and more attentive during these sections of the prayer.

The Communion Rite

The sign of peace may be given at a funeral as at any Mass. Normally the priest is not supposed to leave the sanctuary, but he may do so at funerals. The General Instruction of the Roman Missal (GIRM) permits him to greet "a small number of the faithful near the sanctuary" (154). The sign of peace is designed more to express the peace that does exist among Christians, rather than sorrow, repentance, greeting, congratulation, or condolence. In this case, however, the rubric turns it into an opportunity for comfort.

I try to keep my message on point: "Peace be with you." Not "I'm so sorry" or "I'll keep you in my prayers." There are other occasions for those sentiments. Even so, I find that some from the family use this time to tell me how beautiful the ceremony is. The sign of peace is not meant to be a break in the liturgy, a time for commentary or socializing. It expresses the peace that binds Christians as a prelude to their Holy Communion.

This may sound a little corny, but after I give the sign of peace to the family, I usually go to the coffin and place my hands upon it in silence, offering peace one last time to the remains of the deceased.

Communion is distributed to those who are eligible to receive. At a funeral Mass, some of those present probably do not belong to the Catholic Church or have other reasons that make them ineligible to share communion. Some priests make an announcement before communion, instructing those who cannot receive to remain in their places or to come forward with hands crossed over their breast to signal their desire to receive a blessing instead. Neither the Vatican nor the conference of bishops in the United States has official directives on blessing non-communicants. The practice has been a grassroots idea that surprisingly caught on throughout the United States and in other parts of the world. Many Catholics expect it as an option.

I do not encourage blessings at communion time. I realize that I don't have a lot of support for this position, but I think blessings confuse the purpose of communion. People object that it seems unwelcoming not to let others come forward for something. Perhaps, but we are still excluding them from communion, as our church teaches that we should. The time for a blessing is at the end of Mass or, at a funeral, at the close of the graveside service. If people come forward with arms crossed, I trace the sign of the cross on their forehead, saying nothing, but I do not invite non-communicants to identify themselves. Personally, I think it is more fitting for them to remain in their pew. But I know that not many people agree with me on this.

Some priests give a short explanation for who is welcome to receive communion in a Catholic Church and who is not. The United States Conference of Catholic Bishops has a carefully scripted summary of the church's viewpoint (http://www.usccb .org/prayer-and-worship/the-mass/order-of-mass/liturgy-of -the-eucharist/guidelines-for-the-reception-of-communion.cfm), which appears in many participation aids. It may already be in the pew. If the priest chooses to explain these, he runs the risk of being too short, too long, too imprecise, too apologetic, or too confrontational. If he feels moved to say something, he may direct people to the appropriate page in the participation aid that they have within reach. Or the complete guidelines could be published in a funeral program.

Some parishes include a song after communion. At any Mass, a song may be sung after communion (GIRM 164); one citation says that it is to be sung by everyone (GIRM 88), implying that it is not to be a solo. However, this is when some musicians like to perform the *Ave Maria* or some other devotional song. The OCF makes no mention of any music right after communion, even though some parishes include it as faithfully as any other part of a funeral service. Sometimes mourners augment a song in honor of Mary by having someone present flowers to an image of the Virgin during the music. This has some devotional appeal, but the liturgical books do not promote it, probably because it distracts from the purpose of communion, and it is not an element that directly encourages the full, conscious, active participation of the people (Constitution on the Sacred Liturgy 14).

The communion rite concludes with the prayer after communion. In general these prayers ask God to let the communion that people have received strengthen them for their journey toward eternal life. Or they pray to bring the deceased person to the everlasting joys of resurrection. As at any other Mass, these words prayed aloud by the priest presume that all those who pray along silently have received communion, which is not always the case. There is nearly always some disjunction between the actions just performed and the words of this prayer. If few are receiving communion, it may be more prudent to select a prayer that focuses attention on the salvation of the deceased, rather than on that of the communicants.

The presider has to switch books after this prayer, turning from the Missal to the OCF. The OCF has communion prayers near the back in paragraph 410. I sometimes use one of those for the prayer after communion. That way, when communion is over and I have returned to the chair, I use one book, the OCF, not two, with ribbons set for the prayer after communion and for

> the final commendation. It is also permitted to say the prayer
> after communion at the altar. The priest could read the prayer
> from there and then move to a different location with a different
> book for the final part of the Mass.

If announcements are to be made, they follow the prayer after
communion. For example, if people need to hear instructions
about the procession to the cemetery, the service to take place
there, or any reception or meal following the Mass or the cemetery
service, this is the time. The priest may make these, but someone
else could instead. The ambo should not be used for announcements at any Mass, including a funeral. Sometimes the cantor's
microphone makes a good location.

The Mass is suspended here. There is no final greeting, blessing,
or dismissal. The service concludes at the cemetery. In practice,
some priests, realizing that not everyone is going to the cemetery,
conclude the Mass in the usual way after the final commendation.
But the OCF does not foresee this as an option. It moves seamlessly
from the prayer after communion to the final commendation, to
the cemetery.

If the burial is going to be delayed, or if the body is being trans-
ferred to another state or country for burial, then it makes sense
to conclude Mass in the usual way. The conclusion, however, is
designed to take place at the cemetery.

The Final Commendation

Normally the priest leads the final commendation inside the
church, but he may hold it at the cemetery. There are two possible
reasons why this may happen. One is the unusual circumstance
when the Mass has been celebrated without the body present, as,
for example, when the body has been cremated and interred in
the cemetery before the Mass. In that case, the final commendation
is part of the cemetery service. The Ceremonial of Bishops envisions a second reason why the commendation may be delayed:
the burial is taking place inside the church (833). In that case, the

procession would move to the place of interment inside the building, and the final commendation and rite of committal are com-
bined.

> Some people have unnerved the congregation by mispronounc-
> ing the title of this section. No one has to introduce this cere-
> mony during the Mass, but if anyone does, that person should
> be careful to pronounce the word correctly. It's the final "com-
> mendation." Not the final "condemnation."

The priest goes to a place near the coffin, accompanied by ministers carrying the censer and blessed water if these are to be used.
They are optional in the United States, but always part of the rite
in the Latin original. The priest should be facing the people. Actually, if the presider's chair is near the coffin, the priest need not
move. He could lead the opening invitation to prayer from his
chair, with the assistants nearby.

In some parishes, servers holding cross and candles group
themselves at the opposite end of the coffin. The OCF does not
call for this, probably because the procession has not yet begun.
The assisting ministers hold incense and blessed water if anything,
not candles and cross, and they are to stand near the priest.

At this point, when the ministers are in place for the final commendation, the OCF gives permission for someone to speak "in
remembrance of the deceased" (170). This permission also exists
in the Latin original. Some priests and pastoral ministers prefer
not to include this option, or to limit it to the vigil service. However, families who request it are within their rights because the
official liturgy of the church permits it. Unfortunately, the English
translation of that permission does not accurately carry the intent
of the Latin, which says, "An Episcopal conference may permit
that, according to the custom of the place, after a period of silence,
words of greeting, offered by the relatives of the deceased, may
be delivered." This rubric appears after the priest is standing at the
coffin, and after he has invited people to pray in silence, just before
the sprinkling and incensation. Words "of greeting" are not the

same as words "in remembrance." The original rubric envisions that someone from the family or a friend of the deceased would simply greet those present, thank them for coming, and perhaps invite them to the lunch afterwards. That was it. This permission, however, has mushroomed into a practice that those who composed the post–Vatican II funeral rites would barely recognize.

In English, the rubric permitting someone to speak in remembrance of the deceased was moved from its original position after the invitation to prayer and silence (172) into the position just before these take place (170). Even so, OCF 170 envisions that the priest and ministers are standing near the coffin before the words of remembrance begin. This is widely ignored. The words in remembrance usually happen while the priest is sitting down, a concession that this is going to take a while.

Words in remembrance introduce other moods to the funeral Mass. Some people tell stories that recall happier times. These can put the person's life in perspective at a time when mourners may be focusing on a final prolonged illness, the suffering of the deceased and of the family, and of the many inconveniences and sacrifices sustained in the time leading up to death.

The words in remembrance, however, have become a problem in some Catholic funerals. Parish planners lose control of the length and content of these words. They may offer guidelines, but these are nearly impossible to enforce. The length of the remembrance has sometimes exceeded that of the homily. Sometimes more than one family member wishes to speak, and the time doubles or triples. The Catholic Mass is a carefully balanced liturgical action that keeps its parts in check. Just as an overly long homily can make the Liturgy of the Eucharist feel secondary to the preacher's need to speak, so the public memories of one or more speakers can topple the purpose for which the mourners have come. The Catholic liturgy allows announcements near the end of the service, but the rubrics consistently describe them with the same two qualifiers: "brief" and "if necessary." The pace and flow of the liturgy demand that announcements and words in remembrance be reserved.

Perhaps one factor contributing to the growing custom of increased eulogies is that the church service is the main public event at which the greatest number of mourners will gather. Those involved in parish ministry often complain that their weekend attendance is not higher, and that some people show up only for the most significant church events of the year. Even so, a parish Sunday Mass offers one of the few places where people gather in great numbers in a typical week for a common purpose. Some places of business see the same number of people each day, but usually not gathered at the same time for the same purpose. Those who work at theaters and stadiums are more familiar with the experience that parishes have. Many people do not even hear live music all week unless they come to church. They may not sing outside of Mass. At church they can see many of their friends who share their values all at one time. The church is providing not only a liturgical service but a social network as well. At the time of death, people want to gather. The church provides a venue where this can happen.

There is no other place where mourners can speak publicly about their love for the deceased. The same group who shared connections with a deceased person will not reconvene at city hall or the public square. They may go to someone's home or gather at a bar, but the numbers will be smaller. They may receive cards in the mail, but in person they cannot address a group of people all at once in any other venue except the church where the funeral is taking place. This dynamic has made it appealing, even expected, that someone who really knew the deceased person will speak, even if that person has limited skills in public speaking, cannot organize thoughts succinctly, and wants to share the microphone with others suffering the same loss.

Behind all this hides a misunderstanding of the role of the liturgy. Many people who do not come to church are unfamiliar with liturgical routines. They assume that since they are in a public gathering space that the democratic rules of public gatherings prevail. At a liturgy, however, the Mass takes precedence. It should not be made secondary to other speeches. But what can a person do?

Some parishes have created policies that permit remembrances at the vigil for the deceased, but not at the funeral Mass. This has the advantage of pulling the remembrances outside the eucharistic context, where they can derail the proceedings. Others permit remembrances before the Mass begins. For example, if the funeral is scheduled for 10:00 a.m., words of remembrance may begin at 9:30 or 9:45, preparing people for the funeral Mass. Such a schedule could be included in the obituary: "Remembrances at 9:30 a.m., funeral Mass at 10:00 a.m." Other parishes forbid words in remembrance absolutely. It would help everyone if dioceses developed policies in this regard, and if pastors agreed to support them. In time, word would spread that the local Catholic churches have set guidelines and restrictions on this part of the service. There should be a way to honor the rubric in the OCF, the requests of the mourners, and the demands of the liturgy. Because the custom has spread wide, it will take more than one priest in one parish to control it.

For the final commendation, the priest invites all to pray, and all observe silence. Then he may sprinkle the coffin or the urn with blessed water and incense it. In the United States, the sprinkling with blessed water is discouraged (173) "if the body was sprinkled" at the beginning of Mass. That's right: "if." But the body is always sprinkled at the beginning of this Mass, so many parishes have omitted the sprinkling here as a duplication. The Latin original makes no such restriction. It expects that both sprinkling and incensation will take place at this time.

Meanwhile, musicians lead the song of farewell (174). The OCF offers several options, and composers have written some musical settings for all to sing. Even the most faithful churchgoers on Sundays, however, may be unfamiliar with this repertoire. It may therefore be good to include this music at Sunday worship sometime during the year, or at least rehearse it on Sundays, so that worshipers may become familiar with it. A diocesan liturgy office could encourage all parishes to build a common repertoire of one or more selections from a recommended list of songs of farewell.

The introduction to the OCF calls this music "the high point of the entire rite" (10). It rarely feels so. However, in this moment in the funeral rite the community entrusts the body and soul of the deceased to the hands of God. This part of the ritual used to be called "absolution," but this has been changed because "the purification of the deceased . . . is what the eucharistic sacrifice accomplishes" (Introduction 10). The body must be present for this song of farewell.

In the prayer of commendation (175) the priest commends the departed person to God with the help of the community's prayer.

The deacon invites all to join the procession to the place of committal (176). If there is no deacon, the priest makes the invitation. At this time the OCF calls for the *In paradisum*, one of the most famous and eloquent chants of the traditional funeral liturgy. The English translation in the United States includes a metric version of the words that could be sung to a popular hymn tune (396 E). It is a most fitting way to conclude the service at the church and begin the procession to the cemetery. In reality, however, this text is often set aside, as it may be, in favor of another song that the community knows better and that is felt better to express the faith and hope of those who have suffered this loss.

The rubrics are not clear about which reverences are proper to the altar and the tabernacle as the priest leaves the sanctuary. Normally at the end of Mass he kisses the altar, bows to it (GIRM 90d), and adds a genuflection to the tabernacle if the tabernacle is in the sanctuary (274). At a funeral, however, the Mass is not ending. The Ceremonial of Bishops makes a case that anyone entering or leaving the sanctuary during the course of the Mass makes a low bow to the altar (72), so it seems that that is the rubric that best applies here. After the last words of the Mass (OCF 176) the priest goes from his chair directly to the center aisle, without kissing the altar. He turns, makes a low bow to the altar, and then, without a genuflection, exits.

The OCF does not describe the procession from the sanctuary to the door of the church. Customarily, the same order observed at the beginning is repeated at the end. The ministers and the priest exit first, followed by the coffin and the mourners. Funeral directors customarily move the coffin to the side so that the ministers may exit down a clear aisle. They usually turn the coffin so that the body moves feet first. In the case of cremation, the urn should be carried out with dignity.

At the conclusion of this procession, the coffin is uncovered. If a cross, Bible, or Book of the Gospels has rested on top for the Mass, someone removes it and sets it aside. Similarly, the pall is taken off and stored. The OCF does not call for any ceremony surrounding these gestures. Frequently the funeral directors fold up the pall and hand it to a sacristan or other representative of the local parish. If the cross that was in use is also brought to the graveside, a funeral director may slip it into a pocket at this time.

Sometimes the priest sprinkles the coffin with blessed water before it leaves the church. Some priests hand the sprinkler to concelebrants, family members, and nearby mourners so that all can take a turn. There is no rubric calling for this. In fact, if sprinkling is to happen, it belongs with the final commendation inside the church, rather than at the transferring of the body at the conclusion of the funeral Mass. Perhaps the custom persists because Catholics usually dip their fingers into a holy water stoup before exiting a church, making the sign of the cross. Even that gesture, however, appears in no liturgical book. After one has received Holy Communion, there is nothing more that holy water can do to add to the blessing or consecration of a faithful Catholic.

If a national flag is to cover the coffin again, this action takes place after the pall has been removed, near the door of the church.

When a meal is provided for the mourners, some families prefer to have it follow the Mass and precede the travel to the cemetery. They realize that not everyone will take the time to go to the cemetery, but they would stay long enough to eat. This affords some practical advantages of keeping a large group together for a longer period of time, but it presents certain challenges as well. From the liturgical perspective, the Mass leads directly into the graveside service. Even the travel is intended to be a solemn time of prayer. Inserting a meal between the two is almost like taking a lunch break at a typical Mass between the Liturgy of the Word and the Liturgy of the Eucharist. A meal at this point also presents a challenge to the funeral home staff. They often have committed personnel and vehicles to the entire event, and an intervening meal can add one or more hours to their time on a busy day. The custom of offering a meal provides needed hospitality to mourners, and usually they are better able to relax and enjoy it as the last event of a ritual day.

The length of time between the funeral Mass and the rite of committal may vary in different parts of the country. In some places, the entire funeral takes place rather quickly after death. In other climes, a winter funeral may delay the burial until the ground has sufficiently thawed.

The Rite of Committal

The Procession

A procession forms from the church to the graveside. The OCF includes this among its related rites and prayers (127), and it provides a generous selection of psalms that could be used at this or other times of the rite (347).

The procession is usually a cortege led by motorcycles directing traffic and by the hearse bearing the body of the deceased. Other vehicles join in the procession and, depending on local custom, may flash blinkers as the cortege takes to the streets. Customarily, other drivers not involved with the funeral pull to the side of the road to let the procession pass, out of respect for the deceased. Some passersby visibly stop and pray. Some families choose not to pay for a motorcycle escort, asking everyone to drive on their own to the cemetery at a certain hour.

Employees of funeral escort services agree that the demand for their business has taken a nosedive in recent decades. Fewer people want a formal, escorted procession to the cemetery. Perhaps this reflects either a preference for individual freedom in one's car or the decreased demand for graveside services resulting from the private final disposition of cremated remains.

> Often the funeral home provides a car for me. The arrangement provides someone on the staff an opportunity to network. I respect the need for developing professional and friendly relationships with funeral home personnel, but I usually don't like idle talk between the church and the cemetery. I may be the only priest who feels this way, but I'd rather spend the time in prayer and reflection while in procession. It keeps me focused on my responsibilities. When I reenter the car at the end of the cemetery service, I'm in a more relaxed frame of mind and can more readily enjoy conversation.

Especially in rural America some funeral homes are a short walk to a church. If the pallbearers are able, they may carry the coffin. Others could recite the pertinent psalms. Some parishes have their own cemeteries, and pallbearers could perform a similar service when the main funeral liturgy is over. Cantors could provide singing in procession.

Where these processions take place in cars, passengers usually socialize. They may offer prayers, however, such as the rosary. The parish could provide a booklet with prayers for them to read or an audio recording of psalms recommended for this procession (OCF 347). The parish could even provide a website or a podcast with psalms so that mourners with smartphones could read them or lead others in the same exercise. A Catholic radio station could broadcast the recitation of psalms at a time of day when processions are likely to form. Unlikely as it is for this to catch on, some mourners might appreciate a way to sacralize the time inside the car.

At the Cemetery

At the graveside comes the rite of committal. Normally a priest or deacon presides over this service, but another parish minister or a friend or member of the family may do so (OCF 215). An ordained minister appropriately dresses in alb and stole, but some priests preside over the committal wearing their clergy suit, perhaps a small stole draped around their neck. The color for such a stole comes from the same options as for the vesture at Mass: white, purple, or black. Most probably choose white.

Sometimes the cemetery staff arranges for the service to take place in a chapel or enclosed area near but not at the site of committal. During inclement weather, one can understand the impulse to provide comfort. Even so, having the final commendation take place apart from the grave is not ideal. The actual grave provides the visual references to the purpose for the procession to the cemetery. The cemetery staff commonly erects a tent over the graveside. This helps mourners identify the place for the service and provides shelter from excessive heat, cold, wind, or precipitation.

Pallbearers traditionally carry the coffin from the hearse to the graveside. As in the church, they usually carry the body of the deceased feet first. This continues the image of one's journey of life, feet forward, head up. Employees of the funeral home and of the cemetery usually help position the coffin on a frame, suspended above the vault, which conceals the depth of the grave. Many cemeteries require a vault—not to protect the coffin, but to preserve the appearance of the lawn above the grave. Without a vault, the earth above the coffin collapses more easily, making it more difficult to maintain the grass. Some vaults are sealed in order to protect the coffin, but this is not always required. A concrete vault may close without sealing, thus allowing natural elements to decompose the body.

If cremation has occurred, one or more pallbearers should carry the remains with dignity from the car to the place of committal. The ashes may be placed in a grave, mausoleum, or columbarium, a wall with small recessed compartments specially designed to receive cremated remains.

This brief service may be lengthened (211). For example, sometimes the distance between the church and the graveside is considerable, and a completely different group of mourners from that location arrives for the interment. In that case, the committal may be lengthened with readings from Scripture, songs, or other additional elements.

It takes time for mourners to gather. As they arrive, a minister or employee of the funeral home may need to invite them to draw closer in order to see the grave, hear the words, and participate more actively. The cemetery staff usually provides a few chairs for family or friends who are closest to the deceased or most feeble in health.

The minister opens the ritual with an invitation to prayer. A text is supplied, but similar words may begin the proceedings (216). This gathers the attention of the faithful and creates a spirit of reflection.

Someone may then read a brief passage from the Scriptures indicated at OCF 217. Although not indicated, an assisting minister surely may perform this duty. Sometimes a person from the parish staff or a faithful volunteer makes a good choice for this role. There are several other parts that an assisting minister may lead, so having someone familiar with the service can help diversify the ministries and give the ceremony a more liturgical feel.

The minister says a prayer over the place of committal (218). The circumstance governing the choice of the options supplied is whether the place has been blessed and whether the final disposition of the body is to take place at a later time. In Catholic cemeteries, the whole cemetery has been blessed, so the option without a blessing of the grave is more appropriate there. At other cemeteries, the minister would fittingly say the prayer of blessing.

As many have observed, this prayer of blessing does not call for a visible sign of blessing—no sign of the cross from the minister's hand, no sprinkling with blessed water. The Latin original of the funeral rite, however, includes a notice that the English translation omits: at the conclusion of this prayer the minister may sprinkle blessed water and incense the grave. The minister may also sprinkle and incense the body of the deceased, unless this was done as part of the final commendation at the church (OE 53). Some funeral homes carry a vial of blessed water in the coach in the event that the minister wants to sprinkle the grave but forgot to bring the proper equipment.

If the final disposition of the body takes place at a later time, a different prayer is offered. This is the most common circumstance when the mourners will depart before the coffin is lowered into the earth or secured in a mausoleum.

The committal is to take place at this time, right in the midst of the prayers at the graveside (219). Literally, at this moment, the coffin is lowered into the earth or the remains are placed inside the mausoleum while all the mourners watch and pray. Catholics rarely observe this custom in the United States, but it may be done, and the OCF places quite some emphasis on its importance for Christians: "The act of committal expresses the full significance of this rite. Through this act the community of faith proclaims that the grave or place of interment, once a sign of futility and despair, has been transformed by means of Christ's own death and resurrection into a sign of hope and promise" (209).

I often ask about this when I visit with the family in the days before the funeral. "Would you like to be present when the body is lowered into the earth? The Catholic funeral rite permits and encourages it as a statement of faith." I usually get the response you would expect, "No." Then after a moment more, "No, we don't think so." But every so often I find someone who opens their eyes wide, cocks their head, and asks, "Really? I didn't know you could do that." I had one person angry because I forgot to talk about this, and she found out a week *after* the funeral that being present for the lowering of the coffin had been a possibility. "If only I had known, I definitely would have wanted to be there." Arrangements need to be made with the funeral home and the cemetery, so it takes some advance planning. Some may prefer only to lower the coffin into the vault and consider the job done. That is something, but it is not the same as remaining present in prayer as even the vault is lowered into the earth.

If we are to inter the remains at this point of the service, I explain it to the mourners at the start of the rite of committal. That way they are not completely taken off guard, and, if some have objections, they can turn aside when the time comes. I sometimes lead the mourners in a decade of the rosary as the coffin goes into the earth. It takes just the right amount of time, and it affords some Catholics the comfort of a traditional prayer as they stand together at an emotional moment. If musicians are present, however, they may lead everyone in singing a psalm.

After the minister says the words for the committal, the intercessions follow (220). The minister introduces these, and an assisting minster reads the intentions, as would happen at the prayer of the faithful at a typical Mass. Then all recite the Lord's Prayer (221), and the minister offers the concluding prayer (222).

The prayer over the people concludes the service (223). Many have observed that the liturgical architecture of this segment does not flow very well. The minister asks all to bow and pray for God's blessing, and after some silence the minister says the prayer over the people. Then, when a priest or deacon would normally give the trinitarian blessing, the minister leads the funeral dialogue, "Eternal rest grant. . . ." Finally, a minister who is a priest or deacon says what appears to be another prayer over the people, followed by the trinitarian blessing and the dismissal. It appears as though people are supposed to keep their heads bowed, somewhat awkwardly, through all those preceding elements. They may naturally lift their heads after the first prayer for the funeral dialogue, but that puts them out of the traditional posture for the prayer over the people that follows the dialogue. In Latin, there are simply two components after the Lord's Prayer: a prayer over the people and the funeral dialogue (OE 56). The English translation in the United States has added a few other elements in a way that does not naturally flow. It does add a blessing, however, which the original Latin omits both at Mass and at the cemetery. This blessing brings the liturgy to a more satisfactory close, and helps link the rite of committal back to the funeral Mass. The various elements may feel liturgically bumpy, but they are all striving to bring the service to a close.

A song may conclude the ceremony. As odd as this may seem, a good song can draw people together in a final chorus of praise before they take their leave. A cantor could lead verses to a refrain that people know. A participation aid may include words to sing.

Even one verse of a hymn people know from memory may be enough to end the liturgical services on a strong note.

Signs of Farewell

The liturgy at the graveside allows some freedom, and into that invitation has stepped other customs: military, local, and traditional. If the deceased person is a veteran of the armed forces, military honors may be given at the grave. The OCF does not clearly indicate how military honors are to be made. Often they are done at the conclusion of the rite of committal. This essentially creates two services back to back. In the United States, if the coffin has been draped with a flag, uniformed officers will remove the flag, fold it, and present it to the closest family member of the deceased. The ceremony is impressive. The respect offered the nation's flag normally holds a standard for reverence that even some parish liturgies strive to achieve. Officers totally focused on their duty follow a precise, dignified, and hierarchical routine in which the flag plays the central role. Once the flag has been presented, there may be a twenty-one-gun salute. (The number is the sum of the figures 1+7+7+6, which spell the year of the nation's birth.) Usually it is not twenty-one guns, but three guns firing seven volleys. Then a bugler plays "Taps." Ideally, a bugler plays. Often a recording plays "Taps," sometime through a speaker concealed inside a faux-bugle that a uniformed officer holds to his lips before pressing the on button. Catholic liturgy avoids the use of recorded music, as noted below. The melody for "Taps" uses four notes. The difficulty of finding a musician who can play them live should be an embarrassment to the entire American culture.

Some local graveside customs persist. For example, in at least one part of the country, it is customary to release doves at the conclusion of the service. The birds hold the attention of the mourners and lift their thoughts away from the grave and toward the skies. The Catholic liturgy does not forbid it, but the practice adds another symbol that may vie for attention amid the more important symbols and words of the ceremony. Similarly, some people release gas balloons, especially at the death of a child. The balloons lend a demi-celebratory atmosphere to the conclusion. Once again, they help move people's thoughts away from the grave into the hope of resurrection.

Some may observe other traditions. For example, after the coffin has been lowered into the earth, some people may throw dirt onto it, as is widely practiced among the Jewish people. The custom is not meant to send the message "Good riddance," but rather "I lay you to rest." It has never been officially a part of the universal Catholic liturgy, but then neither is the sharing of flowers from the spray that may cover the coffin. Yet it is not unusual to see a funeral director invite family members to take flowers as a reminder of the day.

Also customary is the presentation of a crucifix. Often at a Catholic funeral, the funeral home has provided the crucifix that rests on top of the coffin for the Mass. Sometimes the family provides its own crucifix, one that has significant relevance to the one who has died. After the ceremony at the graveside, the priest may take the crucifix from the coffin and place it in the hands of the closest family member among the mourners. The gesture appears in no Catholic liturgical book, yet the tradition has remained strong. For this reason, some variations have appeared, such as the placement of multiple crucifixes on the coffin so that multiple members of the family may take one home. The Catholic liturgy shies away from repetitious symbols such as multiple crucifixes on a coffin, so another solution could be a serial placement of different crucifixes at the vigil, the funeral Mass, and the committal. That way only one rests on the coffin at any one time.

Some coffins come affixed with removable corners depicting a religious image. These may be removed and shared with family members after the service, along with or as an alternative to the crucifix. None of this is in the OCF, so one should be careful about multiplying symbols, lest they diminish the traditional ones associated with Catholic funerals.

Other activities have happened at graveside: the playing of a favorite musical recording, a live musician, the telling of stories, or the taking of photos. But the Catholic liturgy envisions that when the prayers are over, the assembled mourners disperse.

Sometimes they stay a while. They visit with friends and family one last time. They pay final respects to the remains of the one who has died. Eventually, they move to their vehicles and depart.

The funeral director sometimes likes to conclude the rite of committal. For example, the representative who has been helping the family may say something like this: "On behalf of the family, I'd like to thank all of you for coming out today. This concludes our service." From the liturgical perspective, there is no such line in the OCF. However, it is somewhat diaconal. It is the kind of remark a deacon would make to let people know where they stand and what to do next. On one hand, it seems to say to the community that the real presider over these events was the funeral director, not the priest. On the other hand, someone has to tell people that they can go home. The liturgical blessing should convey that message, but in reality many people do not understand from it that they may now leave.

> I often find it difficult to judge when to leave the grave and go to the car. I am usually ready to go when I conclude the service, but I don't want people to think I'm disrespectful or that my prayers were not sincere. Upon concluding the prayers, I may say a few words privately to the closest family members, and then slowly walk back to my vehicle, or whatever vehicle transported me. That allows anyone who still wants to see me time to catch up and say what is on their minds.
>
> If there is a meal after the funeral, that gives me additional time to visit with the mourners. In that case, I try to shake the hands of every one of them, if that is feasible, and thank them for offering a fitting conclusion to a person's life.

Musical Selections

The Missal gives some indications about music for the funeral liturgy. The music from a typical Sunday liturgy serves as an adequate guide. The same opportunities for hymns, acclamations, and dialogues that the community sings on Sunday present themselves again at funerals. In addition, there is the song of farewell. The Missal suggests a variety of texts for the entrance and communion chants at a Mass for the Dead. For example, the first suggested entrance antiphon is based on a text from the little-known apocryphal Fourth Book of Esdra: "Eternal rest grant unto them, O Lord, and let perpetual light shine upon them." In Latin, this antiphon begins with the word *Requiem*, meaning "rest." That is the reason one still may hear people speak of a funeral as a Requiem Mass. They are referring to the first word of the entrance antiphon, which gave the entire Mass its name.

However, neither this nor any of the Missal's other entrance antiphons—or its communion antiphons—have yet received treatment from composers that has earned them a position in the popular vernacular repertoire for funerals. Perhaps this should not be surprising. The translations of these antiphons were revised in 2011 with the publication of the third edition of the Roman Missal. It will take composers a while to be inspired to set these antiphons to music, and time for people to sift through the compositions to discern which are the ones that gain wide enough usage to enter the national funeral repertoire.

As it stands, other songs have become staples at Catholic funerals in the United States: "On Eagle's Wings," "How Great Thou Art," and "Shepherd Me, O God," to name a few. Although the possibilities for funeral music are endless, the national repertoire for English-speaking America has remained somewhat narrow. This has the advantage of inviting people to sing songs that they know very well. It actually imitates the preconciliar strategy, which offered one set of chants to be repeated at every funeral, no matter the status of the person who died. Still, a congregation with a more varied repertoire may appreciate singing music that especially fits the circumstances of the departed and the manner of his or her death.

Recorded music is not supposed to be used in Catholic church services (*Notitiae* 3 [1967] 3–4). Some parishes resort to it because they have been unable to recruit musicians. Live music, however, is always preferred and is worth the effort to obtain. The Catholic Church's foundational piety is incarnational—that God took on human form. So we use the things of earth to discover anew the presence of God. We use bread, wine, oil, water, branches, and ashes, as well as the human voice. When a living person is bringing music into the service, the community recognizes another human being who took the time to be present and to share faith in song. Especially at a funeral, recorded music can establish an uncomfortable middle ground between the deceased and the survivors. The music is not really live, and it is not really dead.

In general, songs of a secular nature do not have a place at Catholic liturgy. These can be presented at a meal that follows the service. The music of Catholic worship, however, is integral to the liturgy. It is not something appended to create a veil of beauty. It frames and delivers the words of worship. It has a very specific purpose. Any other music will diminish its impact. The Second Vatican Council's Constitution on the Sacred Liturgy calls the church's musical tradition "a treasure of inestimable value, greater than that of any other art" because song unites with words, making it necessary and integral to the liturgy (112).

Some parishes or funeral homes print a program for each funeral giving a photo of the deceased, the obituary, the Scripture citations, and the songs. This helps all who have come to participate, and it provides a keepsake for the family. If the program includes any copyrighted material, permissions should be obtained and noted. The parish may also use the program as an evangelization tool. It may include contact information: its name, address, website, phone number, and email address, as well as any pertinent notifications about connecting through social media. A program provides a way that family members can remember the parish long after the funeral. Some day they may need a priest or the assistance of the many competent ministers who help at a funeral. If they have an easy way to contact the parish, it will more easily create the bridge.

The Role of Priests

Near the end of the introduction to the OCF, several paragraphs instruct priests about what is expected of them. Priests are to be particularly mindful of non-Catholics or Catholics who seldom come to Mass or who seem to have lost their faith. They are servants of all God's people (18). Their responsibilities include ministering at the side of the sick and the dying, catechizing people on the meaning of Christian death, comforting the family, helping them prepare for the funeral, and fitting the liturgy for the dead into the parish's liturgical life and their own pastoral ministry (25).

Priests really do care about people who die and those who survive them. Some deaths are hard for the priest. He may not only be a minister; he may also be a mourner. He may have lost a close friend in the parish, or a member of his own family. Yet he may be asked to serve as the priest for everyone else, and to tend to his grief in other ways. We are not supposed to have favorites among our parishioners, but we do. Everyone has favorites among the people for whom they are responsible. Although priestly ministry keeps death constantly before our eyes, we still must deal personally with death whenever it occurs in our families or among our friends. Our familiarity with funerals keeps us ever close to the mystery of death.

Funerals are a service that Catholic parishes offer to human society. But they also serve the priest as he prepares for his own death.

Toolbox

3

The Readings

The variety of readings available for funerals reflects the variety of individuals and circumstances of death that require attention. There follows a commentary on all the readings from the Lectionary's Masses for the Dead, detailing the church's beliefs and a scriptural background.

Two charts follow these commentaries, one suggesting circumstances when certain readings could be used, and the other presenting keywords that appear in the readings. The number of the readings comes from the *Lectionary for Mass*.

Beliefs and Commentaries: General

Reading I from the Old Testament (1011)

1. 2 Maccabees 12:43-46

Beliefs: The Catholic custom of praying for the dead has biblical foundations in this passage. Even though this passage was written before Christ, it demonstrates a clear belief in life after death and the value of having the living pray for the dead.

Commentary: Judas Maccabeus was a Judean leader who organized a revolt against foreign invaders. Many of his soldiers died in the resistance, and he honored them by collecting contributions toward a sacrificial offering for the forgiveness of their sins. Unbelievers would have thought this foolish, but he expected the fallen to rise again.

2. Job 19:1, 23-27a

Beliefs: Catholics believe in the resurrection of the body and the second coming of Christ. In this passage Job foreshadows these beliefs when he says, "from my flesh I shall see God," and that his vindicator (redeemer) will come "at last."

Commentary: Satan has wagered with God that Job will lose faith if he loses his family, health, and possessions. God accepts the deal, and in passages like this, the suffering Job shows the unchanging strength of his faith.

3. Wisdom 3:1-9 or 3:1-6, 9

Beliefs: This Old Testament passage foreshadows the Christian belief in life after death. It challenges the viewpoint of unbelievers.

Commentary: This passage acknowledges two schools of thought about death: one that it is "an affliction" and "utter destruction," the other that it represents "peace" and "immortality." To believers, those who suffer before they die are merely "chastised a little" and are tested "as gold in the furnace." (The short form eliminates some of the images in order to tighten the message.)

4. Wisdom 4:7-15

Beliefs: Life is a precious gift even for those who die young. Some people achieve greatness in only a few years. The value of human life is not measured by its length of days.

Commentary: This passage grapples with the mystery of those who die young. It says that an honorable age is not "measured in terms of years" but by "understanding" and "an unsullied life." These traits are just as good as the white hair ("hoary crown") that represents "the attainment of old age." Those who die young are "snatched away" from the wickedness of this world and have become "perfect in a short while."

5. Isaiah 25:6a, 7-9

Beliefs: We believe that God is more powerful than death. Death is the common lot of all humanity, "the web that is woven over all nations," but Isaiah prophesies that God will "destroy death forever."

Commentary: To a people suffering oppression and warfare, Isaiah sends a message of hope. It may appear that death is all around, but "on this mountain"—Jerusalem—God will wipe away tears and remove "the reproach of his people." Prophesying the second coming of Christ, Isaiah looks forward to a day when God will come and people will recognize him as the Savior.

6. Lamentations 3:17-26

Beliefs: The value of life is not measured by one's trials. Even in the face of poverty and loss, "the favors of the LORD are not exhausted." God offers "saving help" to those who hope in the silence of death.

Commentary: This is a song of sorrow bewailing the destruction of Jerusalem and its temple in 587 BC. The singer has "forgotten what happiness is" but still believes that God's mercies "are renewed each morning, / so great is his faithfulness."

7. Daniel 12:1-3

Beliefs: We believe that Christ will come at the end of time to render universal judgment on the living and the dead. "Some shall live forever, / others shall be an everlasting horror and disgrace."

Commentary: A terrible persecution of Jews occurred in the second century BC. Daniel prophesies a message of hope that God will render a final judgment in favor of those who have suffered much for their faith. This passage gave birth to the tradition that Michael the archangel would stand guard at the final judgment.

*Reading I from the New Testament
during the Season of Easter (1012)*

1. Acts of the Apostles 10:34-43 or 10:34-36, 42-43

Beliefs: Jesus rose from the dead and is appointed by God as judge of the living and the dead. During Easter time, we reflect on the resurrection of Jesus, which made possible our own resurrection from the dead. (The shorter version of this reading emphasizes the judgment.)

Commentary: Peter is visiting the house of Cornelius, a Gentile who has summoned him and asked him to instruct his household. Peter details the highlights of Jesus' life and ministry and then explains that the apostles have been commissioned to preach and testify to him. In this context, Peter says things that comfort the bereaved today: Jesus is risen, and he will return as judge.

2. Revelation 14:13

Beliefs: Those who die in the Lord rest with him. God rewards those who have faith and act upon it. During Easter Time we glimpse the eternal life that God has prepared for us in Christ.

Commentary: In a vision, John sees a great multitude worshiping the Lamb. Three angels arrive with messages about those who are redeemed—and those who are not. Afterward, John hears a voice blessing those who die in the Lord, and the Spirit says they will find rest from their labors, for their works—their good deeds—accompany them.

3. Revelation 20:11–21:1

Beliefs: There will be a final judgment rewarding the good and punishing the evil. During the Easter season we proclaim our belief that Christ is risen and ascended and that he will return to judge the living and the dead.

Commentary: John sees a vision of judgment just before his final vision of a new heaven and a new earth. The one seated on the throne judges the dead based on their deeds recorded in scrolls.

4. Revelation 21:1-5a, 6b-7

Beliefs: At the end of time, there shall be no more death. A new heaven and a new earth will be established. During Easter time we celebrate the rising of Christ and the promise of eternal life.

Commentary: This reading comes from the last chapter of the last book of the Bible. The book of Revelation has many vivid and violent images, but it closes with a vision of peace. The old world is passed. A new world comes. There will be no more tears. God makes all things new.

Responsorial Psalm (1013)

1. Psalm 23:1-3, 4, 5, 6

   Beliefs: God will guide the faithful through the dark valley of death to the green pastures of eternal life. God has the power as well as the desire to care for us.

   Commentary: Possibly written by a shepherd who understood the imagery, this psalm imagines that God is the shepherd and the author is the sheep. The psalm proclaims a message of God's provident care of whatever threatens the security of those who pray this text. It is perhaps the most popular psalm in the Bible, and it provides exceptional comfort at the time of death.

2. Psalm 25:6 and 7b, 17-18, 20-21

   Beliefs: After our death, our souls enter eternal life. We lift them to the Lord. Those who await redemption while asleep in death will not be put to shame.

   Commentary: The psalm is prayed by a person who is suffering troubles of the heart, distress, and affliction. This person has faith that God can come to the rescue, and begs for that favor. Although this prayer was written about the concerns of the living, it can be heard as the soul's plea for redemption.

3. Psalm 27:1, 4, 7 and 8b and 9a, 13-14

   Beliefs: God offers salvation to those who seek it. The faithful yearn to spend all the days of their lives with God. They will see the good things of the Lord in the land of the living.

   Commentary: The psalmist has experienced the beauty of the temple and taken comfort there. The temple has become a symbol of the desire to dwell in God's house forever. At the time of death, the brightness of a loved one's life is ended, but Christians believe that God offers eternal light and everlasting life in a heavenly dwelling place.

4. Psalms 42:2, 3, 5cdef; 43:3, 4, 5

   Beliefs: Our souls are on a pilgrimage toward God, and we long to see him face to face. Those who are burdened with cares are consoled by the presence of God.

Commentary: This psalm was composed for pilgrims to sing on their way to the temple. They are thirsty from their travel, but the excitement of reaching the destination keeps them going. We Christians believe we are on a pilgrimage toward God's temple in heaven. Our thirst for the living God will be satisfied at the end of our days when we see him face to face.

5. Psalm 63:2, 3-4, 5-6, 8-9

Beliefs: Our souls yearn to be one with God as much as the hungry and thirsty yearn for food and drink. God's right hand upholds those who cling to him.

Commentary: This psalm was written for those who spend time praying to God in a holy place. They believe in God's power, and they believe that God's goodness is like feeding the hungry with a rich banquet. The psalm was written for the living who hunger for greater union with God, but it expresses our belief that our souls can find ultimate union with God after death.

6. Psalm 103:8 and 10, 13-14, 15-16, 17-18

Beliefs: God is good, and God will care for us in eternity in spite of our unworthiness. Our days are brief, like those of grass or flowers, but God's love is eternal.

Commentary: The psalm is a prayer by those who realize that God gives more than we deserve to receive. God does not deal with us according to our sins, but rather with the love that parents extend to children. At funerals we seek the consolation that God will forgive the sins of the deceased and offer them kindness, mercy, and salvation.

7. Psalm 116:5, 6, 10-11, 15-16ac

Beliefs: God is merciful toward those who suffer. The death of the faithful is precious in God's eyes, and they will walk in the presence of the Lord "in the land of the living."

Commentary: The psalmist has been inhibited by "bonds," has been "greatly afflicted," and has realized with some alarm that no one is dependable. But God remains merciful. Christians are especially taken by the prophetic words that the death of the faithful is precious in God's eyes, and that after death the Lord loosens the bonds of the faithful so that they may walk forever with God in the land of the living.

8. Psalm 122:1-2, 4-5, 6-7, 8-9

Beliefs: The Christian life can be compared to a pilgrimage to Jerusalem, where the faithful may live forever with joy in God's house.

Commentary: This is a song written for pilgrims to sing on their way to Jerusalem. They rejoice as they enter the gates, see others streaming toward the same goal, and behold judgment seats. Prayers for peace are spoken. When Christians reach the end of their earthly journey, they rejoice to enter the gates of heaven.

9. Psalm 130:1-2, 3-4, 5-6ab, 6c-7, 8

Beliefs: At the end of our lives we cry out to God for mercy. We acknowledge that we are sinners, but we trust that God will forgive. Our souls cry to God "out of the depths" of death, yet we hope and trust in his Word.

Commentary: The singer of this psalm is in a situation so desperate that this prayer has to rise "out of the depths." Mindful of personal sin, the psalmist relies on God's forgiveness and mercy. This text was written about a dire situation being faced in life, but Christians pray this psalm as if it were spoken by the souls of the faithful departed. After death our souls will "wait for the LORD / more than sentinels wait for the dawn." We wait with hope that God will redeem us.

10. Psalm 143:1-2, 5-6, 7ab and 8ab, 10

Beliefs: God grants forgiveness to those who pray for it. The redeemed will hear of God's mercy at the "dawn" of eternal life.

Commentary: The psalmist is asking God for a special personal favor. However, the psalmist is guilty of sin and asks for God's mercy. The "soul" thirsts for God, and in this phrase Christians see a prophecy for how the dead cry out to God for forgiveness and the gift of eternal life.

Reading II from the New Testament (1014)

1. Romans 5:5-11

Beliefs: Christ died for us that we might be saved. Even though we are sinners, God loves us. We have hope in eternal life, and hope does not disappoint.

Commentary: Saint Paul is explaining the deep love that God has for us. You might lay down your life for a family member, a close friend, or a good person, but Christ died for us while we were still sinners. If God loved us enough to do that, surely God will save us through the life of his Son.

2. Romans 5:17-21

Beliefs: Sin entered the world through Adam, but grace entered through Christ Jesus, and grace is more powerful than sin. Eternal life is more powerful than death.

Commentary: Paul contrasts the roles of Adam and Christ. Adam's actions affected us all: they brought sin and death into the world. But Christ's actions also affected us all: They brought grace and eternal life to us.

3. Romans 6:3-9 or 6:3-4, 8-9

Beliefs: In baptism we share in the death and resurrection of Christ. As Christ was raised from the dead, we too may live in newness of life.

Commentary: Paul explains the implications of the resurrection of Jesus. He died and rose from the dead. We participate in the mystery of his death and resurrection when we are baptized. Our baptism is a promise that we who have died with Christ may also be raised with him. (The short form focuses the primary images of this passage.)

4. Romans 8:14-23

Beliefs: We are children of God. We suffer that we might be glorified. We await the redemption of our bodies.

Commentary: Paul explains that the Holy Spirit has made us children of God, joint-heirs with Christ—through suffering—to eternal glory. Our sufferings are nothing compared to the glory that is to come. All of creation eagerly awaits renewal. As labor pains precede birth, so our suffering precedes our redemption.

5. Romans 8:31b, 37-39

Beliefs: God loves us, even when others oppose us. Christ died, was raised, and intercedes for us. Nothing will separate us from the love of Christ—not even death.

Commentary: Paul explains how God defends those who belong to him. He handed his own Son over for us, so we can expect God to forgive us even when others condemn us. Nothing can separate us from the love of God in Christ Jesus our Lord.

6. Romans 14:7-9, 10c-12

Beliefs: We belong to the Lord in life and in death. Christ died for this reason. We shall all give an accounting of ourselves for the judgment of God.

Commentary: We have a tendency to judge our neighbor, but it is we who shall be judged. Paul reminds us that we belong to God whether we live or die, and he will judge us at the end of time. We should live not to judge another but for the glory of God.

7. 1 Corinthians 15:20-28 or 20-23

Beliefs: Christ has been raised from the dead. He will come again and will present to God those who belong to him.

Commentary: Saint Paul explains the second coming of Christ. He affirms the resurrection of Christ, who is the "firstfruits" of those who have died. God will bring to life those who have followed Christ. All things—even death—are subject to Christ. (The short form of this reading retains the principal points of Paul's presentation.)

8. 1 Corinthians 15:51-57

Beliefs: When Christ comes again, he will raise the dead and rescue those who are still living. The faithful shall live incorruptible and immortal.

Commentary: Paul offers consolation to those concerned about eternal life. Some Christians were dying before Christ returned; the living did not want the dead to miss out on the promises of the resurrection. Paul says Christ will rescue the living and the dead. Death is swallowed up in the victory of Christ.

9. 2 Corinthians 4:14-5:1

Beliefs: God, who raised Jesus from the dead, will raise up the faithful with him. Our bodies may suffer, but our afflictions produce glory beyond comparison.

Commentary: Paul affirms the resurrection and places suffering in context. He explains that the "outer self" may waste away, but our "inner self" is renewed each day. Suffering is a "momentary light affliction" when compared with the glory that awaits us. We dwell in temporary housing; we await an eternal home in heaven.

10. 2 Corinthians 5:1, 6-10

Beliefs: We await an eternal dwelling in heaven. We try to please God, for we will appear before the judgment seat of Christ.

Commentary: Saint Paul offers consolation to those who realize how short this life is compared with the eternal life that awaits us. He says we may be at home in the body, but "we are away from the Lord." We courageously look forward to going home to the Lord. Christ will judge our actions, so we try to please him while we live.

11. Philippians 3:20-21

Beliefs: Jesus our savior will come again. He will change us to be like his body in glory.

Commentary: Saint Paul tells the Philippians about their future glory in heaven. Although they live in earthly cities, they are—first of all—citizens of the heavenly city. Christ has subjected all things to himself, and with this power he can change our mortal bodies to be like his in glory.

12. 1 Thessalonians 4:13-18

Beliefs: Jesus has risen from the dead. The faithful who have died shall rise again.

Commentary: Some people believe that those who die are gone forever, but St. Paul disagrees. The Lord Jesus will come again. When he does, those who are alive will meet him together with those who have died to live with him for ever.

13. 2 Timothy 2:8-13

Beliefs: If we have died with Christ, we shall also live with him. If we persevere through our sufferings, we shall reign with him.

Commentary: Saint Paul writes to Timothy from prison. His enemies can chain him, but they cannot chain God's word. Paul is confident in this saying: if we have died with Christ we shall also live with him.

14. 1 John 3:1-2

Beliefs: We are children of God. One day we shall be like God, for we shall see him as he is.

Commentary: Saint John tells about the unique relationship we have with God. Others in the world do not know God. But we are God's children now, and "what we shall be has not yet been revealed." But we shall be like God when we see him as he is.

15. 1 John 3:14-16

Beliefs: In love, Jesus laid down his life for us. To love is to participate in God's life.

Commentary: John talks about the relationship between love and eternal life. If we love others, we pass from death to life. Christ laid down his life for us and showed us how to love. We ought to lay down our lives for others.

Gospel (1016)

1. Matthew 5:1-12a

Beliefs: Those who live a virtuous life are blessed, and their reward will be great in heaven.

Commentary: This passage is commonly known as the Beatitudes, one of the most beautiful and memorable sayings of Jesus. It marks the beginning of the Sermon on the Mount, a speech in which he helps his disciples discern how to live. In the Beatitudes Jesus identifies the virtues that make people good disciples, even as he cautions that they will suffer persecution because of him.

2. Matthew 11:25-30

Beliefs: God reveals hidden things to those who are childlike. We come to know God through Jesus, his Son.

Commentary: During the Sermon on the Mount, Jesus addresses words of praise to his Father and words of comfort to his disciples. Jesus praises the Father for revealing himself to Jesus and to the disciples. He invites those who are burdened to come to him and find rest. "My yoke is easy, and my burden light."

3. Matthew 25:1-13

Beliefs: God rewards those who are wise and prepared. Those who act foolishly miss out on heaven's blessings. We do not know the day or the hour when Christ will come for us.

Commentary: Jesus tells this parable near the end of his life. Shortly before his death, he indicates that he will return. He expects that some will be ready to meet him; others will not. He reveals this in an unsettling parable.

4. Matthew 25:31-46

Beliefs: Christ expects us to take care of the needy. He will come again in judgment to reward those who cared for others.

Commentary: Near the end of his life, Jesus tells this parable about the king who returns and separates people as a shepherd separates sheep from goats. He rewards those who feed the hungry, give drink to the thirsty, clothe the naked, welcome the stranger, tend the sick, and visit prisoners. He punishes those who do not.

5. Mark 15:33-39; 16:1-6

Beliefs: Jesus died on the cross for us. He is risen from the dead.

Commentary: Mark tells the story of the death and resurrection of Jesus. This is probably the oldest narrative of the event. Even in his agony, Jesus quotes from the psalms. Signs and wonders convince a centurion that he is the Son of God. Women carrying spices to the tomb discover that it is empty except for a mysterious figure who announces that Jesus has been raised. (The short version tells only of the death of Jesus.)

6. Luke 7:11-17

Beliefs: Jesus has power over life and death. He demonstrated this by raising the dead to life. God can still raise the dead to eternal life.

Commentary: Jesus is moved by the sorry situation of a widow whose only son has died. He commands the young man to "arise"—foreshadowing his own resurrection. The people realize that Jesus is a great prophet, and word of him spreads.

7. Luke 12:35-40

Beliefs: Jesus will come again when people do not expect him. He will reward those servants who await his return.

Commentary: Jesus urges his disciples to be constantly faithful, for they do not know when he will come again. Those who have served others will find that Jesus will be waiting on them instead.

8. Luke 23:33, 39-43

Beliefs: Jesus was crucified for us. He forgives the sinner and offers eternal salvation.

Commentary: Saint Luke is the only writer who reports the conversation between Jesus and the criminals crucified with him. One criminal recognizes that Jesus is innocent and calls him by his first name. Jesus promises that this man will be with him in paradise.

9. Luke 23:44-46, 50, 52-53; 24:1-6a or 23:44-46, 50, 52-53

Beliefs: Jesus died on the cross for us and rose from the dead.

Commentary: Saint Luke says an eclipse of the sun darkened the earth from noon to 3 p.m. on the day Jesus died. He tells of Joseph, who took the body down and laid it in a new tomb. Women bringing spices the next day discovered the tomb was empty. Two men announced to them that Jesus had been raised. (The short version tells only of the death of Jesus.)

10. Luke 24:13-35 or 24:13-16, 28-35

Beliefs: Jesus rose from the dead and appeared to his disciples. We continue to experience his presence in the Eucharist.

Commentary: On the evening of the day Jesus rose from the dead, two disciples walk to Emmaus. Jesus joins them, but they do not recognize him. He explains the Scriptures to them. They ask him to stay with them. When he breaks bread, they recognize him—and he vanishes from their sight. (The short version abridges the story.)

11. John 5:24-29

Beliefs: Those who believe in Jesus have eternal life. The dead will hear the voice of the Son of God, and they will live.

Commentary: In a controversy with fellow Jews, Jesus reveals the message of the resurrection: those who believe will rise from death to life. They will hear the voice of the son of Man and come up out of the tombs.

12. John 6:37-40

Beliefs: Jesus came down from heaven to raise us up on the last day. All those who believe in the Son of God have eternal life.

Commentary: Jesus begins his discourse on the bread of life with remarks about his mission. God has sent him for the purpose of salvation. Those who believe in him shall have eternal life, and he will raise them on the last day.

13. John 6:51-59

Beliefs: Jesus is the living bread come down from heaven. Those who share the Eucharist will live forever.

Commentary: Jesus reveals the mystery of the Eucharist in a discourse to the crowds. He came down from heaven for them, just as manna came from heaven for their ancestors in the desert. Jesus will remain with those who eat his flesh and drink his blood.

14. John 11:17-27 or 11:21-27

Beliefs: Jesus is the resurrection and the life. Those who believe in him will live.

Commentary: At the death of Lazarus, Jesus visits with Martha and Mary. Before he raises Lazarus from the dead, he reveals to them the mystery of death and life: that he is Lord of all, and that those who believe will never die. (The short form compresses the conversation.)

15. John 11:32-45

Beliefs: Jesus has power over life and death. He showed this by raising Lazarus from the dead.

Commentary: Shortly before his passion, Jesus learns of the death of his friend Lazarus. He goes to the home of Martha and Mary to console them, to instruct them, and to startle the crowd by raising Lazarus from the dead. Many came to believe in him because he demonstrated his authority over death.

16. John 12:23-28 or 12:23-26

Beliefs: Death leads to life, as surely as buried grain becomes wheat. Those who live for Christ preserve themselves for eternal life.

Commentary: Shortly before his passion begins, Jesus helps the disciples understand about resurrection. He says a grain of wheat produces fruit only if it dies. He will rise again, and so will his followers. "Where I am, there also will my servant be." (The short form of this reading omits references to Jesus' hour and the Father's glory.)

17. John 14:1-6

Beliefs: Jesus died to prepare a place for his followers. He will come back again and take them to himself. Jesus is the way, the truth, and the life.

Commentary: Seated with his disciples at the Last Supper, Jesus gives a final instruction about his mission. He will die, but he is going to prepare a place for those who follow him. When Thomas asks him the way, he says, "I am the way and the truth and the life."

18. John 17:24-26

Beliefs: Jesus is our Savior. He prays that those who follow him may see the glory of the Father.

Commentary: Seated at the Last Supper with his disciples, Jesus ends the meal by offering a prayer to his Father. He prays for those who followed him, "that they may see my glory that you gave me" and "that the love with which you loved me may be in them."

19. John: 17-18, 25-39

Beliefs: Jesus was crucified for our salvation. He entrusted the church to the care of his mother. He left us baptism and the Eucharist to sustain us.

Commentary: Saint John tells the story of the death of Jesus. On the cross he entrusts his mother and the disciple whom he loves to their mutual care. As he dies, he breathes his last, handing over the Spirit. A soldier punctures his side with a lance. Blood and water flow out. Joseph of Arimathea and Nicodemus lay him to rest.

Beliefs and Commentaries: Funerals of Baptized Children

Reading I from the Old Testament (1017)

1. Isaiah 25:6a, 7-9

Beliefs: We believe that God is more powerful than death. "The Lord GOD will wipe away / the tears from all faces."

Commentary: To a people suffering oppression and warfare, Isaiah sends a message of hope. It may appear that death is all around, but "on this mountain"—Jerusalem—God will wipe away tears and remove "the reproach of his people." Prophesying the second coming of Christ, Isaiah looks forward to a day when God will come and people will recognize him as the Savior.

2. Lamentations 3:22-26

Beliefs: The value of life is not measured by the length of life. Even in the face of a tragic loss of a child, "the favors of the LORD are not exhausted."

Commentary: This is a song of sorrow bewailing the destruction of Jerusalem and its temple in 587 BC. The singer has "forgotten what happiness is" but still believes that God's mercies "are renewed each morning, / so great is his faithfulness."

Reading I from the New Testament during the Season of Easter (1018)

1. Revelation 7:9-10, 15-17

Beliefs: Salvation comes from God. All the redeemed will worship him. God will wipe away every tear.

Commentary: Saint John describes a vision of heaven. He sees a numberless throng worshiping God. Those who have endured strife are freed from their cares. "They will not hunger or thirst anymore, nor will the sun or any heat strike them. . . . God will wipe away every tear from their eyes."

2. Revelation 21:1a, 3-5a

Beliefs: At the end of time, God will dwell with his people. He will wipe away every tear from their eyes. During Easter time we celebrate the rising of Christ and the promise of eternal life.

Commentary: This reading comes from the last chapter of the last book of the Bible. The old world is passed. A new world comes. There will be no more tears, "no more death or mourning, wailing or pain." God makes all things new.

Responsorial Psalm (1019)

1. Psalm 23:1-3, 4, 5, 6

   Beliefs: God will guide the faithful through the dark valley of death to the green pastures of eternal life. God has the power as well as the desire to care for us.

   Commentary: Possibly written by a shepherd who understood the imagery, this psalm imagines that God is the shepherd and the author is the sheep. The psalm proclaims a message of God's provident care for all the little lambs.

2. Psalm 25:4-5ab, 6 and 7bc, 20-21

   Beliefs: God is a Savior, filled with compassion and kindness. God can preserve the souls he receives.

   Commentary: This psalm is a prayer in time of distress. Those who do not understand God's ways pray "teach me your paths." They remind God of his goodness and ask to be remembered in this time of loss. The souls of the just wait for the Lord.

3. Psalms 42:2, 3, 5cdef; 43:3, 4, 5

   Beliefs: Our souls are on a pilgrimage toward God, and we long to see him face to face. Those who are burdened with cares are consoled by the presence of God.

   Commentary: This psalm was composed for pilgrims to sing on their way to the temple. We Christians believe that from our birth we are on a pilgrimage toward God's temple in heaven. Our thirst for the living God will be satisfied when we see him face to face.

4. Psalm 148:1-2, 11-13a, 13c-14

   Beliefs: God deserves the praise of all creation, the young and the old.

   Commentary: This psalm is a song of praise to God who rules over all. All creation above and on the earth is summoned to give God praise—even the young, "the children of Israel, the people close to him."

Reading II from the New Testament (1020)

1. Romans 6:3-4, 8-9

Beliefs: In baptism we share in the death and resurrection of Christ. As Christ was raised from the dead, we too may live in newness of life.

Commentary: Paul explains the implications of the resurrection of Jesus. He died and rose from the dead. We participate in the mystery of his death and resurrection when we are baptized, even at a very young age.

2. Romans 14:7-9

Beliefs: We belong to the Lord in life and in death. Christ died for this reason.

Commentary: Saint Paul reminds us that we belong to God throughout our lives and after death. This is true no matter how briefly we live.

3. 1 Corinthians 15:20-23

Beliefs: Christ has been raised from the dead. He will come again and will present to God those who belong to him in baptism.

Commentary: Saint Paul affirms the resurrection of Christ, who is the "firstfruits" of those who have died. God will bring to life those who have been baptized as his followers, no matter how young they are.

4. Ephesians 1:3-5

Beliefs: God chose us to be his adopted children through Jesus Christ. A baptized child will always be a member of God's family.

Commentary: Saint Paul gives praise to God for all the blessings we have received. God chose us to be holy and adopts us through baptism.

5. 1 Thessalonians 4:13-14, 18

Beliefs: Jesus has risen from the dead. The baptized who have died shall rise again. Even though we grieve the loss of a child, we have hope.

Commentary: Saint Paul explains that God raised Jesus from the dead. God will bring with Jesus "those who have fallen asleep."

Gospel (1022)

1. Matthew 11:25-30

   Beliefs: God reveals hidden things to those who are childlike. We experience God's presence in the miracle of childbirth. God lightens the burden of our losses.

   Commentary: During the Sermon on the Mount, Jesus addresses words of praise to his Father and words of comfort to his disciples. Jesus praises the Father for revealing himself to those who are like children. He invites those who are burdened to come to him and find rest.

2. Mark 10:13-16

   Beliefs: The kingdom of God belongs to those who are like children. Jesus loved children.

   Commentary: The disciples try to keep children away from Jesus, but he says, "Let the children come to me." He offers the kingdom of God to them, and urges all to accept the kingdom as children do. Jesus embraced children and blessed them.

3. John 6:37-40 (6:37-39)

   Beliefs: Jesus came down from heaven to raise us up on the last day. He will not lose any of us—not even the smallest child.

   Commentary: God sent Jesus for the purpose of salvation. He will raise up on the last day all those whom the Father gave him.

4. John 6:51-58

   Beliefs: Jesus is the living bread come down from heaven. Those who share the Eucharist will live forever.

   Commentary: Jesus talks about the Eucharist. He will remain forever with those who eat his flesh and drink his blood.

5. John 11:32-38, 40

   Beliefs: Jesus has power over life and death. He comforted the family of Lazarus by raising him from the dead.

   Commentary: Jesus has learned of the death of his friend Lazarus. He goes to the home of Martha and Mary to console them in their loss, to instruct them, and to raise Lazarus from the dead.

6. John 19:25-30

> *Beliefs*: Jesus was crucified for our salvation. He entrusted the church to the care of his mother.

> *Commentary*: Saint John tells the story of the death of Jesus. On the cross he entrusts his mother and the disciple whom he loves to their mutual care. As he dies, he breathes his last, handing over the Spirit.

Beliefs and Commentaries:
Funerals of Children Who Die before Baptism

Reading I from the Old Testament (1023)

1. Isaiah 25:6a, 7-8

> *Beliefs*: We believe that God is more powerful than death. "The Lord GOD will wipe away / the tears from all faces."

> *Commentary*: To a people suffering oppression and warfare, Isaiah sends a message of hope. It may appear that death is all around, but "on this mountain"—Jerusalem—God will wipe away tears and remove "the reproach of his people." Prophesying the second coming of Christ, Isaiah looks forward to a day when God will come and people will recognize him as the Savior.

2. Lamentations 3:22-26

> *Beliefs*: The value of life is not measured by the length of life. Even in the face of a tragic loss of a child, "the favors of the LORD are not exhausted."

> *Commentary*: This is a song of sorrow bewailing the destruction of Jerusalem and its temple in 587 BC. The singer has "forgotten what happiness is" but still believes that God's mercies "are renewed each morning, / so great is his faithfulness."

Responsorial Psalm (1024)

Psalm 25:4-5ab, 6 and 7b, 17 and 20

> *Beliefs*: God is a Savior, filled with compassion and kindness. God can preserve the souls he receives.

> *Commentary*: This psalm is a prayer in time of distress. Those who do not understand God's ways pray "teach me your paths." They

remind God of his goodness and ask to be remembered in this time of loss. The souls of the just wait for the Lord.

Gospel (1026)

1. Matthew 11:25-30

Beliefs: God reveals hidden things to those who are childlike. We experience God's presence in the miracle of childbirth. God lightens the burden of our losses.

Commentary: During the Sermon on the Mount, Jesus addresses words of praise to his Father and words of comfort to his disciples. Jesus praises the Father for revealing himself to those who are like children. He invites those who are burdened to come to him and find rest.

2. Mark 15:33-46

Beliefs: Jesus died on the cross for us. He is the Son of God.

Commentary: Mark tells the story of the death of Jesus. Signs and wonders convince a centurion that he is the Son of God. His disciples mourned the loss of the one they loved, and they arranged a respectful burial for him.

3. John 19:25-30

Beliefs: Jesus was crucified for our salvation. He entrusted the church to the care of his mother.

Commentary: Saint John tells the story of the death of Jesus. On the cross he entrusts his mother and the disciple whom he loves to their mutual care. As he dies, he breathes his last, handing over the Spirit.

Beliefs and Commentaries: Readings outside these Selections

Mourners sometimes ask if they are limited to the readings that the lectionary supplies for the funeral Mass. Although there is no clear answer to this, the OCF assigns to conferences of bishops the authority to expand components of the ritual wherever options exist: "In drawing up particular rituals for funerals, it shall be up to the conferences of bishops: . . . to add different formularies of

the same type whenever the Roman Ritual provides optional formularies" (OE 22/3). Furthermore, the Introduction to the Lectionary for Mass says that its selection of readings for the Masses for
the Dead "provides many texts that can be of assistance in adapt-
ing such celebrations to the situation, circumstances, and concerns
of the particular groups taking part" (86). It does not explicitly
limit the choices to these selections.

At issue are two passages that many of those who are dying (as
well as the mourners) find especially appropriate. The first can be
found as the first reading on Friday of the Twenty-Ninth Week in
Ordinary Time in Year II; the second is the second reading on the
Thirtieth Sunday in Ordinary Time in Year C.

1. Ecclesiastes 3:1-11 (*Lectionary for Mass* 453)

> *Beliefs*: There is a time for everything under heaven. There is a time
> to be born and a time to die.

> *Commentary*: Many people find the honesty of this passage especially
> consoling. They have reached a point in life when they realize that
> they will not live forever, and they have accepted the inevitability
> of death within a sense of Christian hope.

2. 2 Timothy 4:6-8, 16-18 (Lectionary for Mass 150)

> *Beliefs*: The Christian will face struggles but will overcome them all
> in Christ.

> *Commentary*: Saint Paul reflects on the difficulties of his career, but
> he has confidence that a crown of righteousness awaits him because
> the Lord has stood by him. Many people remember a slightly dif-
> ferent translation than the one in the lectionary: "I have fought the
> good fight. I have run the race."

Circumstances for Selecting Readings

The chart below lists a series of purposes for which certain readings may be more appropriate than others.

	OT LM 1011	NT E LM 1012	Psalm LM 1013	NT LM 1014	G LM 1016	OT 1017	NT E 1018	Psalm 1019	NT 1020	Gospel 1022	OT 1023	Psalm 1024	G 1026
To affirm the resurrection of Jesus		1											
To affirm the resurrection of the body	1, 2, 3, 6	2	1, 2, 3, 4, 5, 7, 8	3, 8, 11	11, 12	1, 2	1, 2	1, 2, 3, 4	1, 2, 3, 4, 5	1, 2, 3, 4, 6			
To affirm the second coming of Christ	5, 7	3, 4	7		3								
To console those worried about the salvation of the deceased	1	3	1, 2, 6, 9, 10	1, 2, 7, 8, 12	8, 13, 14, 18	1, 2	1, 2	1, 2, 3, 4	1, 2, 3, 4, 5	1, 2, 3, 4, 6	1, 2	1	1, 2, 3
To show that God has mercy on sinners			2, 6		8, 19								
To honor one who lost his or her life while rescuing another			1, 15		4, 9, 19								
To honor someone who has experienced war or extreme strife	1, 5, 6, 7	2	1, 2	4, 5, 13, 15	1, 5, 8								

Purpose	OT LM 1011	NT E LM 1012	Psalm LM 1013	NT LM 1014	G LM 1016	OT 1017	NT E 1018	Psalm 1019	NT 1020	Gospel 1022	OT 1023	Psalm 1024	G 1026
To honor those who prayed and served their parish church			3, 4, 5, 7, 8	3, 6, 11, 14	1, 3, 11, 12, 13, 16, 17, 18								
To honor someone for whom baptism or Easter were important				3, 14	5, 9, 10, 15, 16, 19								
To honor someone for whom the eucharist was important					10, 13, 16, 17								
To encourage prayer for the dead	1		6, 10										
To honor one who has suffered personal losses	2, 3, 5, 6	4	7, 9	5, 9	2								
To honor one who has suffered an unfair illness	2, 3, 4	4	4, 9, 10, 13	2, 6, 14, 15					5				

	OT LM 1011	NT E LM 1012	Psalm LM 1013	NT LM 1014	G LM 1016	OT 1017	NT E 1018	Psalm 1019	NT 1020	Gospel 1022	OT 1023	Psalm 1024	G 1026
To honor a baptized child						1, 2	1, 2	1, 2, 3, 4	1, 2, 3, 4, 5	1, 2, 3, 4, 5, 6			
To honor a child who died before baptism											1, 2	1	1, 2, 3
To honor one who died young	4		6	8, 10, 12, 14	5, 6, 9, 14								
To honor one who suffered an unexpected death					3, 6, 7, 15					5	1, 2	1	1, 2, 3
To honor one noted for his or her virtue	4, 7	2, 3	3, 5	6, 7, 10, 11, 15	1, 4, 7, 11, 12, 18								
To honor one who served the community					4, 7								
To honor one whose life was a difficult journey	4, 8, 9, 10	1, 2, 4, 5, 9, 12, 13	2, 10, 17										

Keywords for Selecting Readings

The first column of the charts below list a number of words that appear in the Lectionary's reading for funeral Masses, grouped by categories. The right column shows where these keywords appear in the lectionary.

Sometimes in conversation with a grieving family, the minister will hear certain words that recur. These can be checked against the chart to enter into the Scripture readings in a different way.

Keywords: Belief	Lectionary numbers
acquits, acquittal	1014.2, 1014.5
angels, archangel	1014.5, 1014.12, 1016.4, 1016.10, 1019.4
anoint, anointed	1012.1, 1013.1, 1016.5, 1019.1
baptism	1012.1, 1014.3, 1020.1
believed, believes	1012.1, 1013.7, 1016.12, 1016.14, 1016.15, 1016.19, 1022.3, 1022.5
change, changed	1014.8, 1014.11
chosen	1012.1, 1014.13
deed(s)	1012.3, 1016.10
faithful, faithfulness	1011.3, 1011.6
forgiveness	1012.1, 1013.9
glory, glorify, glorified	1013.5, 1014.3, 1014.4, 1014.9, 1014.11, 1014.13, 1016.4, 1016.6, 1016.10, 1016.15, 1016.16, 1016.18, 1020.1, 1022.5
grace	1011.3, 1014.2, 1014.9
heaven(s), Paradise	1012.3, 1012.4, 1014.9, 1014.10, 1014.11, 1014.12, 1016.1, 1016.2, 1016.3, 1016.8, 1016.12, 1016.13, 1016.16, 1016.18, 1018.2, 1019.4, 1020.4, 1022.1, 1022.3, 1022.4, 1026.1
immortality	1011.3, 1014.8
judged, judgment	1012.3, 1013.10, 1016.11
name	1013.5, 1013.8, 1016.18, 1019.4
power(s)	1012.1, 1013.5, 1014.3, 1014.5, 1014.11, 1016.11, 1020.1
procession	1013.4, 1019.3
redemption	1013.9, 1014.4
sanctuary	1013.5, 1016.5, 1026.2
save(d), savior, salvation	1011.5, 1013.3, 1013.6, 1013.7, 1014.1, 1014.11, 1014.13, 1016.8, 1016.16, 1017.1, 1018.1, 1019.2, 1023.1, 1024

Belief *continue*

Keywords: Belief	Lectionary numbers
sins, sinners	1013.2, 1013.6, 1014.1, 1014.2
testify, testified	1012.1, 1016.19
truth	1011.3, 1016.17, 1016.19, 1019.2, 1024
victor, victory	1012.4, 1014.8
will	1013.10, 1016.12, 1020.4, 1022.3

Keywords: Body	Lectionary numbers
blood	1016.13, 1016.19, 1022.4
bone	1016.19
ears	1013.9
eye(s)	1011.2, 1011.3, 1012.4, 1013.7, 1014.8, 1016.10, 1016.15, 1016.18, 1018.1, 1018.2, 1022.5
face(s)	1011.5, 1013.3, 1013.4, 1016.9, 1016.15, 1017.1, 1019.3, 1023.1
flesh	1011.2, 1013.5, 1016.13, 1022.4
foot, feet	1013.8, 1014.7, 1016.15, 1016.15, 1022.5
hand(s)	1011.3, 1013.5, 1013.10, 1014.5, 1014.9, 1014.10, 1016.15, 1018.1, 1022.2
head	1016.19, 1022.6, 1026.3
heart(s)	1013.2, 1016.10, 1016.17
knee	1014.6
legs	1016.19
lips	1013.5
loins	1016.7
mouth	1013.5, 1016.19, 1022.6, 1026.3
side	1013.1, 1016.19, 1019.1
sleep	1011.7
soul(s)	1011.3, 1011.4, 1011.6, 1013.1, 1013.2, 1013.4, 1013.5, 1013.9, 1013.10, 1017.2, 1019.1, 1019.2, 1019.3, 1023.2, 1024
tear(s)	1012.4
tongue	1014.6, 1018.1
touch	1011.3, 1022.2
voice	1012.2, 1013.9, 1016.5, 1016.9, 1016.11, 1016.15, 1016.16, 1018.1, 1018.2, 1026.2
walk, walked	1013.7, 1014.10, 1016.10

Keywords: Communication	Lectionary numbers
book	1011.7, 1012.3
conversing	1016.10
inscribed	1011.2
quarreled	1016.13, 1022.4
record	1011.2
scroll(s)	1012.3
speak	1012.1, 1016.6
word(s)	1011.2, 1011.7, 1013.9, 1014.12, 1016.10, 1016.11
write	1012.2
written	1011.2, 1011.7, 1012.3

Keywords: Family	Lectionary numbers
adoption	1014.4, 1020.4
ancestors	1016.13, 1022.4
boys	1019.4
bride	1012.4
bridegroom	1016.3
brother(s)	1014.15, 1016.4, 1016.14, 1016.15, 1022.5
children	1012.1, 1013.6, 1014.4, 1014.14, 1016.1, 1019.4, 1022.2
descendant	1014.13
dwell, dwelling	1012.4, 1013.1, 1013.3, 1014.9, 1014.10, 1016.17, 1018.2, 1019.1
father	1013.6, 1014.4, 1014.14, 1016.2, 1016.4, 1016.9, 1016.11, 1022.1, 1026.1
friends	1013.8
heirs	1014.4
home	1014.10, 1016.14, 1016.19, 1022.6, 1026.3
house	1013.1, 1013.3, 1013.4, 1013.4, 1013.8, 1016.7, 1016.17, 1019.1, 1019.3
husband	1012.4
inherit	1016.1
little ones	1013.7
maidens	1019.4
mother	1016.6, 1016.19, 1022.6, 1026.2, 1026.3
oneself, self	1014.6, 1014.9, 1020.2

Family *continue*

Keywords: Family	Lectionary numbers
relatives	1013.8
sister	1016.15, 1016.19, 1022.6, 1026.3
son(s)	1012.4, 1014.4, 1016.2, 1016.6, 1016.19, 1022.1, 1022.6, 1026.1, 1026.3
tribes	1013.8
virgins	1016.3
widow	1016.6
women	1016.9, 1016.10, 1026.2

Keywords: Food	Lectionary numbers
banquet	1013.5
bread	1016.10, 1016.13, 1022.4
cup	1013.1, 1019.1
drank, drink	1012.1, 1016.4, 1016.13, 1022.4, 1026.2
eats, ate	1012.1, 1016.13, 1022.4
famine, hunger, hungry	1014.5, 1016.1, 1016.4, 1018.1
food	1016.4, 1016.13, 1022.4
fruit	1016.16
parched	1013.5, 1013.10
satisfied	1013.5, 1016.1
table	1013.1, 1016.7, 1019.1
thirsting, thirst(s), thirsty	1012.4, 1013.4, 1013.5, 1013.10, 1016.1, 1016.4, 1016.19, 1018.1, 1019.3, 1022.6, 1026.3
wedding, wedding feast	1016.3, 1016.7

Keywords: Nature	Lectionary numbers
air	1014.12
blooms	1013.6
brightly	1011.7
cave	1016.15, 1022.5
clouds	1014.12
creation, creature	1014.4, 1014.5
darkness	1013.1, 1016.5, 1016.9, 1019.1, 1026.2
depth, depths	1013.9, 1014.5

Nature *continue*

Keywords: Nature	Lectionary numbers
dust	1011.2, 1011.7, 1013.6
eclipse	1016.9
field	1013.6
fire	1012.3
firstfruits	1014.4, 1014.7, 1020.3
flower	1013.6
goats	1016.4
grain	1016.16
grass	1013.6
ground	1013.10, 1016.16
heat	1018.1
height	1014.5, 1019.4
hind	1013.4, 1019.3
Lamb	1018.1
land	1013.3, 1013.7, 1013.10, 1016.1, 1016.5, 1016.9, 1026.2
lead	1011.2
light	1013.3, 1013.4, 1019.3
mountain	1011.5, 1013.4, 1016.1, 1017.1, 1019.3, 1023.1
oil	1013.1, 1016.3, 1019.1
palm	1018.1
pastures	1013.1, 1019.1
pool	1012.3
rock	1011.2
sea	1012.3, 1012.4
shadow	1013.5
sheep	1016.4
shine	1011.7
sky	1012.3
splendor	1011.7
spring	1012.4
stars	1011.7
stone	1016.5, 1016.9, 1016.15, 1022.5, 1026.2
tree	1012.1
valley	1013.1, 1019.1
water(s)	1012.4, 1013.1, 1013.4, 1013.5, 1016.19, 1018.1, 1019.1, 1019.3

Nature *continue*

Keywords: Nature	Lectionary numbers
wheat	1016.16
wind	1013.6
wings	1013.5

Keywords: Object	Lectionary numbers
altar	1013.4, 1019.3
chains	1014.13
chisel	1011.2
cloth, clothed, clothes, gird	1014.8, 1016.4, 1016.5, 1016.7, 1016.9, 1016.15, 1026.2
crown	1011.4
door	1016.3
furnace	1011.3
gall	1011.6
gift, gifts	1012.4, 1014.2, 1016.18
gold	1011.3
harp	1013.4, 1019.3
lamps	1016.3, 1016.7
lance	1016.19
reed	1016.5, 1026.2
robe(s)	1016.5, 1018.1
rod	1013.1, 1019.1
seat, seats	1013.8, 1014.6, 1014.10
spices, myrrh, aloes	1016.5, 1016.9, 1016.19
sponge	1016.5, 1016.19, 1026.2
staff	1013.1, 1019.1
tent	1014.9, 1014.10
throne	1012.3, 1012.4, 1016.4, 1018.1, 1018.2
trumpet	1014.8, 1014.12
veil	1011.5, 1016.5, 1016.9, 1017.1, 1023.1, 1026.2
web	1011.5, 1017.1, 1023.1
wine	1016.5, 1016.19, 1022.6, 1026.2, 1026.3
wormwood	1011.6
yoke	1016.2, 1022.1, 1026.1

Keywords: Occupation	Lectionary numbers
appointed	1012.1
centurion	1016.5, 1026.2
citizenship	1014.11
collection	1011.1
council	1016.9, 1026.2
guardian	1011.7
guide(s)	1013.1, 1019.1, 1019.2
judge(s)	1012.1, 1014.6, 1019.4
labor(s)	1012.2, 1016.2, 1022.1, 1026.1
merchants	1016.3
prince	1011.7
repose, rest	1011.4, 1012.2, 1013.1, 1016.2, 1019.1, 1022.1, 1026.1
reward	1011.1, 1016.1
ruler(s)	1011.1, 1016.10
sentinels	1013.9
servant	1013.10, 1016.7, 1016.16
shepherd	1013.1, 1016.4, 1018.1, 1019.1
soldiers	1011.1, 1016.8
teach	1016.1, 1019.2, 1024

Keywords: Person in Bible	Lectionary numbers
Adam	1014.7, 1020.3
Bildad	1011.2
Cleopas	1016.10
Daniel	1011.7
David	1013.8, 1014.13
Devil	1012.1, 1016.4
Elijah	1026.2
James	1016.5, 1026.2
Job	1011.2
John	1012.2, 1012.3, 1012.4, 1018.1, 1018.2
Joseph	1016.9

Person in Bible *continue*

Keywords: Person in Bible	Lectionary numbers
Joseph of Arimathea	1016.19, 1026.2
Joses	1026.2
Judas Maccabee	1011.1
Lazarus	1016.14, 1016.15
Martha	1016.14, 1016.15
Mary	1016.5, 1016.19, 1022.6, 1026.2, 1026.3
Mary Magdalene	1016.5, 1016.14, 1016.15, 1022.5, 1022.6, 1026.2, 1026.3
Mary the wife of Clopas	1016.19, 1022.6, 1026.3
Michael	1011.7
Moses	1016.10
Nicodemus	1016.19
Peter	1012.1
Pilate	1016.9, 1016.19, 1026.2
prophet(s)	1012.1, 1016.6, 1016.10
Salome	1016.5, 1026.2
Simon	1016.10
Thomas	1016.17

Keywords: Place	Lectionary numbers
building(s)	1013.8, 1014.9, 1014.10
city	1012.4, 1016.6
gate(s)	1013.8, 1016.6
nation(s)	1011.5, 1011.7, 1012.1, 1016.4, 1017.1, 1018.1, 1023.1
paths	1013.1, 1013.2, 1019.1, 1019.2, 1024
refuge, shelter	1013.2, 1013.3, 1018.1, 1019.2, 1024
temple	1013.3, 1016.9, 1018.1
walls	1013.8

Keywords: Suffering	Lectionary numbers
afflicted, affliction	1011.3, 1013.2, 1013.7, 1014.9
afraid	1013.3
alarm	1013.7
anguish	1014.5
bonds	1013.7
burden	1016.2, 1022.1, 1026.1
chastised	1011.3
corruptible, corruption	1014.4, 1014.8
crimes, criminal	1013.6, 1014.13, 1016.8
crucified	1014.3, 1016.5, 1016.8, 1016.10, 1016.19
deny	1014.13
desire	1011.4
destroy, destruction	1011.3, 1011.5, 1014.10, 1017.1, 1023.1
disappoint	1014.1
discouraged	1014.9
disgrace	1011.7
disobedience	1014.2
distress	1011.7, 1013.2, 1014.5, 1024
downcast	1011.6, 1016.10
escape	1011.7
evil	1013.1, 1016.1, 1019.1
fails	1013.10
fallen	1011.1
fear	1013.3, 1013.6, 1016.6, 1016.8
foes	1013.1, 1019.1
forsaken	1016.5, 1026.2
futility	1014.4
grieve	1014.12, 1020.5
healing	1012.1
homeless	1011.6
horror	1011.7
ill	1016.4
iniquities	1013.9

Suffering *continue*

Keywords: Suffering	Lectionary numbers
labor pains	1014.4
lifeless	1013.5
longs	1013.4, 1019.3
lose, lost	1011.6, 1016.12, 1022.3
low, lowly	1012.3, 1013.7, 1014.11
mourn(ed), mourning	1016.1, 1011.7, 1012.4, 1018.2
naked, nakedness	1014.5, 1016.4
oppressed	1012.1
pain	1012.4, 1018.2
passed away	1012.4, 1018.2
peril	1014.5
persecuted, persecution	1014.5, 1016.1
pines	1013.5
pity	1013.3, 1016.6
pleading	1013.10
poor, poverty	1011.6, 1016.1
prison	1016.4
punished	1011.3
reproach	1011.5, 1017.1, 1023.1
rescue	1013.2, 1019.2, 1024
seek	1013.3, 1013.5
shame	1013.2, 1019.2, 1024
sting	1014.8
stranger	1016.4
suffer, suffering(s)	1013.2, 1014.4, 1014.13, 1016.10
supplication	1013.9
sword	1014.5
tears	1011.5, 1017.1, 1018.1, 1018.2, 1023.1
troubled, troubles	1013.2, 1016.15, 1016.16, 1016.17, 1022.5, 1024
wailing	1012.4, 1018.2
want	1013.1, 1019.1
wasting away	1014.9

Keywords: Time	Lectionary numbers
age	1011.4
beginning, foundation	1012.4, 1016.4, 1016.18, 1020.4
dawn, daybreak	1013.9, 1013.10, 1016.9
day(s)	1013.1, 1013.3, 1013.6, 1013.10, 1016.3, 1018.1, 1019.1
early	1011.4, 1016.5, 1016.10
end	1012.4, 1014.7
evening, night	1016.10, 1016.19, 1018.1, 1026.2
first day	1016.5, 1016.9, 1016.10
four days	1016.14, 1016.15
hour	1016.3, 1016.7, 1016.11, 1016.16
last day	1016.12, 1016.14, 1022.3
midnight	1016.3
morning	1011.6, 1017.2, 1023.2
noon	1016.5, 1016.9, 1026.2
third day	1012.1, 1016.10
three o'clock	1016.5, 1016.9, 1026.2
years	1011.4, 1013.1, 1019.1

Keywords: Virtue	Lectionary numbers
blessed	1011.3, 1012.2, 1016.4, 1016.7, 1020.4, 1022.2
boast	1014.1
bounty	1013.3
care, cared	1011.3, 1016.4
childlike	1016.2, 1022.1, 1026.1
clean of heart	1016.1
comforted	1016.1
compassion	1013.2, 1013.6, 1019.2, 1024
console	1014.12
courage, courageous	1013.1, 1013.3, 1014.10, 1019.1, 1026.2
elect	1011.3
excellent	1011.1

Virtue *continue*

Keywords: Virtue	Lectionary numbers
faithful(ness), fidelity	1013.4, 1013.7, 1013.10, 1014.13, 1017.2, 1019.3, 1019.4, 1023.2
favor(s)	1011.6, 1017.2, 1020.4, 1023.2
festival	1013.4, 1019.3
freedom	1014.4
glad, gladness	1013.4, 1016.1, 1019.3
good, goodness	1012.1, 1013.1, 1013.2, 1013.8, 1014.10, 1019.1, 1019.2, 1024
gracious	1013.6, 1013.7, 1016.2, 1022.1, 1026.1
great	1012.3
holy	1011.1, 1011.3, 1012.4
honorable	1011.4
hope, hoping	1011.3, 1011.6, 1014.1, 1014.4, 1014.12, 1016.10, 1020.5
innocent	1011.4
integrity	1013.2, 1019.2
joy	1013.4, 1019.3
just, justice	1011.3, 1011.4, 1011.7, 1013.6, 1013.7, 1013.10
kind, kindness	1013.1, 1013.2, 1013.5, 1013.6, 1013.9, 1019.1, 1019.2, 1024
learned	1016.2, 1022.1, 1026.1
love(d)	1011.3, 1011.4, 1014.1, 1014.5, 1014.14, 1014.15, 1016.18, 1016.19, 1020.4, 1022.6, 1026.3
loveliness	1013.3
meek	1016.1, 1016.2, 1022.1, 1026.1
mercy, mercies, merciful	1011.3, 1011.6, 1013.6, 1013.7, 1013.10, 1016.1, 1017.2, 1023.2
no partiality	1012.1
noble	1011.1
obedience	1014.2
peace, peacemakers	1011.3, 1012.1, 1013.8, 1016.1
perfect	1011.4
pious	1011.1
prosper	1013.8
rejoice(d)	1011.5, 1013.8, 1016.1, 1017.1, 1023.1
revered	1013.9

Virtue *continue*

Keywords: Virtue	Lectionary numbers
righteous, righteousness	1016.1, 1016.4, 1016.9, 1016.18
stouthearted	1013.3
thanks, thanksgiving	1013.4, 1013.8, 1014.9, 1019.3
trust, trustworthy	1011.3, 1013.10, 1014.13
union	1014.3
uprightly, uprightness	1012.1, 1013.2, 1019.2
virtuous	1016.9
wait(s)	1013.2, 1013.3, 1013.9, 1019.2
welcomed	1016.4
wise	1011.7, 1016.2, 1016.3, 1022.1, 1026.1
works	1012.2, 1013.10
worthy	1011.3

Sample Homilies

The following are a few homilies I preached during the calendar year in which I wrote this book. I chose them not for their quality, but for their diversity. These will give you some idea of how I approach preaching at funerals. For the purposes of this book, in all cases I have changed the name of the person who had died.

> I delivered this homily at the funeral of an older man who lived
> near the church, but of whom I was unaware until he was dying.
> His adult son had also recently died of an illness. I reflected on
> my visit to the home, the Scriptures of the Mass, the grief of the
> family, and the season of the year. I encouraged a spirit of hope.

On behalf of all of us at St. Anthony's, I express my heartfelt
condolences to the family and friends of José. It was clear from
my visit to his home how many people were close to him and how
much they loved and respected him. He was receiving medical
and personal care, surrounded by many signs of faith and love.
That kind of attention does not happen by accident. It happens
after a lifetime of faith in God, love for family, faithfulness in
friendships, and the building of a home that is much more than a
house, but a place where people can gather together, grow strong,
and enjoy one another's company.

In his Second Letter to the Corinthians, St. Paul compares our
body to a dwelling place that is wasting away. When your house
grows old, you get to know all the places where it sags, leaks, and
creaks. But it is your home, so you still love it. The same is true of
the bodies of our friends. As they grow old, they also grow weak,
but we still love them even with the parts that don't work as well
as before.

Saint Paul says not to worry about this because "if our earthly
dwelling, a tent, should be destroyed, we have a building from
God, a dwelling not made with hands, eternal in heaven" (2 Cor
5:1). The same God who so miraculously made us and brought us
into human life can miraculously remake us and bring us to eternal
life.

Jesus said as much to his disciples: "In my Father's house there
are many dwelling places. . . . If I go and prepare a place for you,
I will come back again and take you to myself" (John 14:2-3). Jesus
and the Father are one, so he knew well about the eternal home
that awaited him, and he wanted to implant that same assurance
into the hearts of his disciples. He made this statement on the

night before he died, the day we commemorate tomorrow, Holy Thursday.

It is never easy to suffer the death of someone we love, but we have a special opportunity for hope when the funeral of a faithful Christian comes during Holy Week. Family and friends find comfort in the meaning of this week and the words that Jesus spoke when he knew his own death was imminent. You all have suffered grave losses—both of José and of his son, Carlo—in a short space of time. But these events took place at a time of year when even the calendar tries to offer words of consolation. On these days we recall not only the death of Jesus but his promise of eternal life. In the midst of your suffering, know that Christ and his mother have walked this way before you. They understood what it was like to face death and to lose a beloved son. May you find comfort in your faith, and may angels accompany José to an eternal dwelling place in heaven.

I gave the following homily for a man whose widow did not want a funeral Mass, just a ceremony at the cemetery. I therefore designated a weekday Mass later that month for the repose of this man's soul. I invited his widow to come. She was interested but ultimately did not join us. Because this was a regular daily Mass, and because no family was present, I kept this homily especially short. But I wanted to do homage to a faithful member of the parish.

Mike's death came as a surprise to all of us. After a freak car accident, he spent many weeks in hospital care and lost his battle to regain his health. Mike was so full of life that it is hard to think of him gone. In his final days he brought into our lives a great concern for him—which was so unlike him. He lived each day wanting to bring us happiness. His jokes and stories are legendary. Even if you'd heard them before, they would always bring a smile to your face. You could tell that he got great pleasure out of bringing laughter to you. It gave his life purpose.

At the Last Supper, Jesus spoke his final words to his disciples in order to give their life purpose. He knew that they would face days of doubt and loss, but he wanted them to have great peace. His purpose was to share the unity he possessed with the Father, so that the disciples might have union with him. His last words to them before offering his final prayer to the Father were these: "In the world you will have trouble, but take courage. I have conquered the world" (John 16:33).

Perhaps Mike's greatest message to us was the message he gave at the end. In the world you will have trouble. Take courage. Be sustained with laughter, faith, friends, and love. You will have all you need in the face of life's troubles to live in the peace of Christ.

I usually do not go back to my former parishes for funerals unless it is for someone whose funeral I would be attending anyway. In this case, I'd known "Thomas" since my time in the seminary. When his wife died a few years earlier, I was on sabbatical and unable to celebrate the funeral—even though I was their pastor at that time. Because I had known them both for so many years, and because I missed his wife's funeral, I very much wanted to reconnect with the family. I felt as though I were giving a homily for both Thomas and his wife.

Margaret is the reason I got to know Thomas. When I was in college I worked for a local hardware store not because I knew anything about hardware, which I did not, but because my pastor knew the owner. Margaret worked there. She knew the business, and she knew how hopeless I was in the shop. But she helped me. She was experienced, wise, and funny, and she shined on your day like the rising sun. She introduced me to Thomas, who was friendly to me when we first met and stayed that way to the end. I got to meet the rest of the family, too. I was the organist for their daughter's wedding in 1974. Years later I came to St. Regis as a priest, and one of the many joys I had here was renewing my old friendship with Thomas and Margaret. One of the many sorrows was witnessing Margaret's roller-coaster battle with cancer. I was on sabbatical when Margaret died, and I missed her funeral by one day. It broke my heart not to be here. But if you look up the words "broken heart" in a dictionary, you'll find a picture of Thomas. He loved Margaret. He needed her. Even after her death, Margaret never left his side. Thomas had some difficult days, and sometimes he made your days difficult too. It was as if he needed to share his misery, so that we could understand what it was like and have compassion. Thomas had been through a lot. He spent years in proud military service with the US Navy. He helped out at church and with the Knights of Columbus. He worked with his hands as a laborer. He was a tough guy, but his family warmed his heart.

Family life is both enriching and difficult, and even St. Paul seemed to understand that. In his letter to the Romans he talks about the special role that children have in families. They are not slaves; they are loved. They will suffer, but they will also receive a future of possibility. Paul says this is true of our relationship with God, whom we can call Father, just as Jesus did. Paul writes, "We are children of God, and if children, then heirs, heirs of God and joint heirs with Christ, if only we suffer him so that we may also be glorified with him" (Rom 8:16-17). Saint Paul was a child of God, too, so he knew all about love and suffering. He wrote, "I consider that the sufferings of this present time are as nothing compared with the glory to be revealed for us" (v. 18). Paul saw his upcoming death as a kind of adoption, a future of possibility with his true Father, God.

At the Last Supper, Jesus prayed for his disciples, calling upon God with the same title St. Paul later used: "Father," Jesus prayed, "those whom you gave me are your gift to me. I wish that where I am they also may be with me, that they may see my glory that you gave me" (John 17:24). Jesus wanted his disciples with him as one happy family. He never abandoned those who placed their trust in him. He knew they would suffer, but his disciples were like his children—God's "gift" to him, Jesus called them—and he wanted them with him forever.

Thomas was both a son of God and a father of a family. Like any father, he wanted happiness for himself and for the kids who were God's gift. Today we entrust Thomas to the hands of his Father in heaven. We pray that his reunion with Margaret may erase the physical and emotional pains he endured. May Thomas experience peace and joy forever. Whenever we experience loneliness, grief, and suffering, let us recall the words of St. Paul. Those sufferings are as nothing compared with the glory to come. Like a good father, Thomas would want that hope to comfort us all our days.

I did not know this man, but he used to be in the parish and had relatives here. He was an ophthalmologist. I wanted to mine some pertinent images. I almost went overboard with them, but I couldn't resist. He had some rough days with his business, and the family especially wanted to include a reading from the book of Job.

When I was seven years old I nearly lost my left eye in an accident in my own backyard. The doctor who put three stitches in my eye and saved my vision at St. Luke's Hospital back in 1960 was named Padfield. Since then I've been through glasses and contacts and readers and trifocals and progressives. I've even had cataract surgery in that same eye, followed up by not one but two YAG treatments. Like all of you, I treasure the gift of sight.

Dr. Harold dedicated his life to helping people see. He started his career in mathematics, and he was successful, but he yearned for something more and took up the practice of medicine. For almost thirty years he practiced ophthalmology. We describe people like him as someone with a good heart. It's not fair that the very heart that helped many other people get a better life is the heart that failed Dr. Harold last Sunday in Garden City.

He had other worries—both personal and professional. In some ways he was like the hero in one of the most enigmatic books of the Old Testament, the book of Job. Job was a just man enjoying a happy life when all of a sudden his familiar world collapsed around him. He lost his possessions, his family, and his friends. He entered a dialogue with some of his acquaintances to try to make sense out of the sorrows that befell him, and ultimately he had a one-on-one conversation with God. At the end, Job's fortunes were restored. A pivotal moment comes early in the book, the passage we heard as the first reading today. In conversation with Bildad, Job reveals that he may have lost many physical benefits, but he never lost his faith. He knows in the end, somehow, some way, God will take care of him. He says, "I know that my Vindicator lives, / and that he will at last stand forth upon the dust; / Whom I myself shall see." Like someone with a good ophthalmologist, Job says, "my own eyes, not another's shall behold him; / And from my flesh I shall see God" (Job 19:25-27). Christians see in Job's statement a prophecy of Jesus Christ, who will come at last to stand upon the earth and make right again everything that once was wrong.

Dr. Harold was a husband and a father, a student and a teacher, a doctor and a patient. He will be missed by family, patients, and professional colleagues. He was looking forward to a new beginning in Garden City. It did not work out the way he had in mind.

When Jesus arrived at the tomb of his friend Lazarus, people knew his reputation as a miracle worker. On this occasion, of all the miracles that Jesus had worked, what impressed them the most was the way he healed those who could not see. They said behind Jesus' back, "Could not the one who opened the eyes of the blind man have done something so that this man would not have died?" (John 11:37). Jesus then raised his eyes to heaven and prayed.

My brothers and sisters, we have lost a good man. At times like this we are tempted to focus only on loss—as did the friends of Job. But when Jesus gave sight to the blind, he gave them spiritual sight as well. That is what we need today. We put our lives in the hands of the divine healer, the Vindicator who will stand forth upon the dust. We pray that through the faith we share especially in our times of loss, we may give others the gift of sight.

Handouts for Mourners

Here are some handouts you may share with those for whom you minister. These are also available for download from Liturgical Press: www.litpress.org/light-in-the-darkness.

Going to Confession

The death of a significant person in life naturally stirs up powerful memories. Grief is strong because love was deep. Loss feels frightening because presence brought comfort.

You will remember some events that make you smile and others that fill you with remorse. You will recall times of love and times of anger—with the same person.

Perhaps you have some regrets. There were some words you never said, some actions you never performed. Perhaps you wanted a better relationship that always seemed just beyond your reach.

The death of a significant person helps each of us reevaluate who we are, whom we love, how we act, and what we believe.

If this is a time that you would like to express sorrow, the Catholic Church offers you a safe way to do it: going to confession.

Confession is a short prayer service between a Catholic and a Catholic priest. If it has been a while since you have been to confession, or even if you have never been, you may find that now is a good time for this experience.

In confession you tell the priest what you are sorry for. You may be sorry for things that you said and did. You may be sorry for things you did not say and did not do. The priest is required to hold in confidence everything that you say.

After you confess your sins the priest will give you absolution. Through the ministry of the church, the priest prays that God will give you pardon and peace.

Pardon and peace.

He will minister to you, giving you a way to say that you're sorry, and a way to hear that you have been forgiven.

The regular times for confession are posted on your parish website, in the bulletin, or on a sign outside the church. Or you may call the parish office for information. When you go to see the priest, you may confess anonymously or face-to-face.

You may also arrange a time to visit with the priest in person. Contact him and ask when it may be convenient. The appointment will give you a target date to complete your reflection, as well as a more leisurely atmosphere in which a priest can help you explore your thoughts.

If you are a non-Catholic Christian, you may go to a priest for confession if you do not have recourse to a minister of your own church or ecclesial community, if you ask on your own initiative, and if you believe what Catholics believe about confession. If the diocesan bishop has established specific norms in a case like yours, the priest will follow them.

In this time of grief, you will find many thoughts rising up, some that may surprise you. You may be coming to a greater understanding of the main themes of your life.

By making a confession now, you may transition from the past to the future with a sense of joy, hope, and forgiveness.

When to Contact the Parish
about a Funeral

Someone you love is dying. Maybe it's even you.

If you would like to arrange a Catholic funeral, you may contact your local parish at any time. Each Catholic parish offers a ministry for the dead, and you will find someone there with experience to help you make your plans.

Which parish do you contact? Normally, you contact the parish closest to the residence of the one who is dying. All parishes have boundaries designating the foremost area in which its ministers offer pastoral care. Many people, however, choose to belong to a parish different from the one in whose boundaries they live. If Catholics register with a parish, they will have their names and contact information on record, and they will find a more ready welcome at times like this.

It is never too early to make this contact. Some people are under the mistaken impression that the time to contact a priest is when the person has reached the final day or two of life. In the past, a priest came to anoint a person near death in a sacrament called Extreme Unction, meaning last anointing. Many people still refer to it as "the last rites."

However, the anointing has migrated from its position at the end of life to a place earlier in one's illness. When an illness is grave, when a person has reached a certain age when they are more susceptible to illness, or when a person faces surgery, the time has probably arrived for a priest to offer the sacrament of the anointing of the sick.

The most important sacrament to give a person who is dying is communion under its special form, viaticum. The time to contact a priest, deacon, or communion minister is when the person is dying, but is still conscious enough to renew baptismal promises and can swallow. If a priest comes to administer viaticum, he adds the apostolic pardon, granting a plenary indulgence from the Apostolic See. This means that the person not only experiences forgiveness of sins, but also cancellation of the punishments attached to them.

A priest may also hear the person's confession. If you would like this to happen, contact a priest when the person is still able to review life and express sorrow for sins.

A priest's ministry has the greatest impact when he can converse with the sick person and offer the sacraments of confession and the anointing of the sick. You help the priest most if you contact him while the sick person's condition still permits this ministry.

As death draws near to the one you love, a good priest would love to be present, but sometimes he cannot, due to other responsibilities. Any other minister—a deacon, a communion minister, or some other parish leader—may be able to come and lead the prayers for the dying. Or the prayers for the dead.

After death has occurred, in some parishes the priest handles all the local funeral arrangements. In other parishes, someone else may be assigned to the task. Whoever answers the phone at the parish office will know. Or you may review the parish website for pertinent information.

The death of a Catholic creates a void in the lives of family and friends. The local Catholic parish will want to help you through the time of grief and into a period of hope.

What Should a Catholic
Know about Cremation?

The Catholic Church permits cremation. For a number of reasons the church prefers the burial of the body, but it does permit the celebration of a funeral with cremated remains.

Among the reasons in favor of burial of the body are these:

- Seeing the body confronts people with the mystery of life and death.

- The body naturally recalls stories of faith, family, and friendship, the words a person spoke, the deeds a person performed.

- Although we have virtual electronic friendships, people best encounter another person through the body.

- The body experienced the sacraments—being washed in baptism and anointed in confirmation, and by eating and drinking the body and blood of Christ in communion.

- The body is destined for the glory of the resurrection.

- The final care of the body demonstrates dignity for the whole person.

- Burial imitates the burial of Jesus' body, and thus constitutes another layer of discipleship.

If a Catholic chooses cremation, the church prefers that the final disposition of the remains be in a public place, such as a cemetery.

Many survivors make other arrangements: they retain the ashes at home, divide them among family members, or scatter them to the elements. The Catholic Church disapproves of these practices.

According to the Vatican's Congregation for the Doctrine of the Faith, the conservation of ashes in one's home is not permitted, nor may they be scattered in the air, on land, or at sea. Ashes may not be preserved in mementoes such as jewelry (*Ad resurgendum cum Christo*).

The careful placement of ashes honors the remains of the deceased in the same way that burial of the body does. Furthermore, it gives a permanent place where future generations may visit to remember, and where the person's name can be honorably etched.

The Catholic Church also prefers that the final disposition of the ashes take place as soon as possible after cremation has happened. This will protect the remains from accidental or deliberate abuse.

Some crematoriums have a place where the family may gather during the process. If a family desires to be together, they may spend the time offering suitable prayers of thanksgiving and hope, such as Psalms 23, 25, 42, 51, 93, 114 and 115:1-12, 116, 118, 119, 121, 122, 123, 126, 130, 132, or 134.

There are three possibilities for the sequence of events. Here they are in order of preference:

1. The body of the deceased is present for the vigil service and the funeral Mass, and cremation happens before the committal at the cemetery. In this case, the body may be placed first in a ceremonial coffin that will not be interred, and then removed from it for the cremation.

2. The cremation and committal take place before the funeral Mass. In this case, the cremated remains are interred in a cemetery or mausoleum, and then the mourners gather for the Eucharist.

3. The cremation takes place before any of the funeral rites begin, and the cremated remains are present for the vigil, the Mass, and the committal.

Whenever the ashes are presented in public for the funeral services, they should be treated with the same dignity and respect offered a human body. The container should be dignified, and the pallbearers should carry it with honor. Because of the compact nature of the ashes, someone may be tempted to carry it more casually. It is all that remains of a human being. It deserves respect.

Letter to Families concerning Financial Offerings

Dear brothers and sisters in Christ,

I am very sorry to learn of a death in your family. At St. Anthony Catholic Church, we will strive to give you our best pastoral care in this hour of difficulty.

Deacon Tom Powell and I will provide leadership for the services. Cathy Hernandez in our office will help arrange music and ministers at the church for a solemn and sincere Christian funeral.

People often ask about an appropriate gift to the church for these services. This is what people normally offer:

St. Anthony Parish	$150
Clergy	$125
Organist	$125
Cantor	$100
Total	$500

We can distribute these funds if you wish to write one check to St. Anthony Parish. Or our friends at the funeral home can include your offering to us in their arrangements with you.

These are not fees. Any gift will be gratefully received. May God bless you in this time of loss.

In Christ,
Rev. Paul Turner
Pastor

Words in Remembrance— Crafting What You'd Like to Say

The Catholic funeral rites permit someone to speak words in remembrance at the vigil for the deceased and at the funeral Mass. Many families want someone—or several persons—to speak to the assembled mourners. The liturgy of the church permits one.

Less is more. These words are a very small part of the entire funeral liturgy, and they should not divert the attention of the faithful from the common prayers being shared. For the sake of the funeral liturgy, if someone is speaking at Mass, that person should come prepared and aware of the purpose of these words within the flow of the entire service.

If you are going to make some remarks, you have a noble opportunity to help people through their grief. Here are some tips to bear in mind:

- Write out what you want to say. And stick to your script when you speak.

- Keep it short. If you go over 500 words, you are in danger of drawing more attention to yourself and less to Christ, who is the center of the funeral liturgy.

- Find out where you are supposed to stand, and test the microphone before the funeral begins. Ideally, you should not stand at the ambo, which is reserved for the reading of Sacred Scripture. Your microphone may be the one that the song-leader uses, for example.

- Find out when you are supposed to speak. Whether you are speaking at the vigil for the deceased or at the funeral Mass, your remarks may come near the end of the service. In some parishes, you may be asked to speak before the service begins. Speak with the person arranging the funeral liturgy. Be sure you know when to step forward.

- Remember that people are going to hear a lot of words at the funeral. They will hear prayers carefully prepared by the Catholic Church for such occasions. They will hear a homily that the preacher has prepared. They will sing songs that will touch their hearts. Most importantly, they will hear passages of Sacred Scripture. Although you have some dear memories to share, the Scriptures bear the primary responsibility for forming lives.

- The Catholic funeral ritual permits you to speak, but originally the liturgy called your talk "words of greeting," not "words in remembrance." The original concept is that you would greet the assembly on behalf of the family, thank them for coming, that sort of thing. Originally, it was not designed to be anything more than a courteous expression of gratitude focused on the mourners, not on the person who has died.

- You are not responsible for giving a complete biography. If you have more than 500 words you want to share, perhaps you could post it as a video on the web. That will actually broaden your audience beyond those who can attend the funeral. And your words will last a much longer time. Ask about having a link printed in a funeral booklet or on the parish website.

- Pray about what you will say, and let your words come from a heart of faith. You will contribute to the overall memories forged by those who attend a Catholic funeral.

The Procession to the Cemetery

As you enter your cars to drive to the cemetery, you participate in an important part of today's funeral.

The procession bridges two periods of prayer—one at the church and the other at the place of committal. The procession imitates the journey of life, the passage of time, the leaving of one destination and arriving at the next.

Usually the procession takes the most direct route. In some traditions the cars drive past the home of the deceased, as if to offer a final farewell.

You may use your time in the car in various ways—in conversation with other mourners, in silence, or in prayer.

If you want to talk with others, here are some questions you may want to ask:

- What was the highlight of the funeral?

- What words from the Scripture readings struck you?

- When you think back on the homily, what was the best part? Are there some words that you want to remember?

- Did some of the music move you? Which song? How did you feel about it? What words do you remember from that song?

- What about the ritual actions? Did anything strike you about what the ministers did? The decorations in the church? The actions that were performed? The holy water? The incense?

If you'd like to pray while you're in the car on your way to the cemetery, you have many options.

If someone would like to lead the rosary, you may recite it en route.

If someone would like to read something from Scripture, you may find a Bible on someone's cellular device, or you may search the web for Bible passages.

For example, if you are able to locate the book of Psalms, here are some that you might find appropriate: Psalms 23, 25, 42, 51, 93, 114 and 115:1-12, 116, 118, 119, 121, 122, 123, 126, 130, 132, or 134.

However you spend your time, you will be in a vehicle with people experiencing grief in different ways. You will help one another while you are traveling, as we all aim to do on the road of life.

The Rite of Committal with Lowering of the Coffin

When you arrive at the cemetery today, you will participate in a brief prayer service that will include the lowering of the coffin into the earth.

Over the past few days, you have lost someone you loved, and you have had to adjust your life to a new reality. The funeral services aim to help mourners move from one stage of grief to another, even as the remains are transported from one place to another.

The final stage may be the most emotional. At the cemetery, you have arrived at the last farewell.

You will hear words of welcome, a brief passage from Scripture, and prayers associated with burial.

Then the one you love will be lowered into the earth like the planting of a seed. For Christians, death is filled with the hope of resurrection. Jesus of Nazareth compared his own death to a grain of wheat that would fall to the earth and die before it produces much fruit.

The service then continues with additional prayers and a blessing.

As you stand above the grave today, you profess your faith that the fruit produced by this life has only begun to flower. Memories and stories will keep the person alive for those of us on earth, and your loved one awaits the promise of eternal life for those who lived in faith. To stand above the grave is to stand in faith, hope, and love that death does not have the final word.

Perhaps the most difficult part of the day is to leave the cemetery. Yet you will leave with a sense that you have offered all you can to honor a person whose life inspired you. A funeral moves mourners through some necessary stages of grief. It does not end the grief, but it will give you new ground where you can stand to face a different future.